At Home on the Prairie
The Houses of Purcell & Elmslie

By Dixie Legler · Photographs by Christian Korab

An Archetype Press Book

CHRONICLE BOOKS
SAN FRANCISCO

HOUSES SHOULD NOT BE CLAMPS TO FORCE US TO THE SAME THINGS THREE HUNDRED AND SIXTY-FIVE DAYS IN THE YEAR ... BUT THEY SHOULD BE BACKGROUNDS FOR EXPRESSING OURSELVES IN THREE HUNDRED AND SIXTY-FIVE DIFFERENT WAYS IF WE ARE NATURAL ENOUGH TO DO SO.

William Gray Purcell

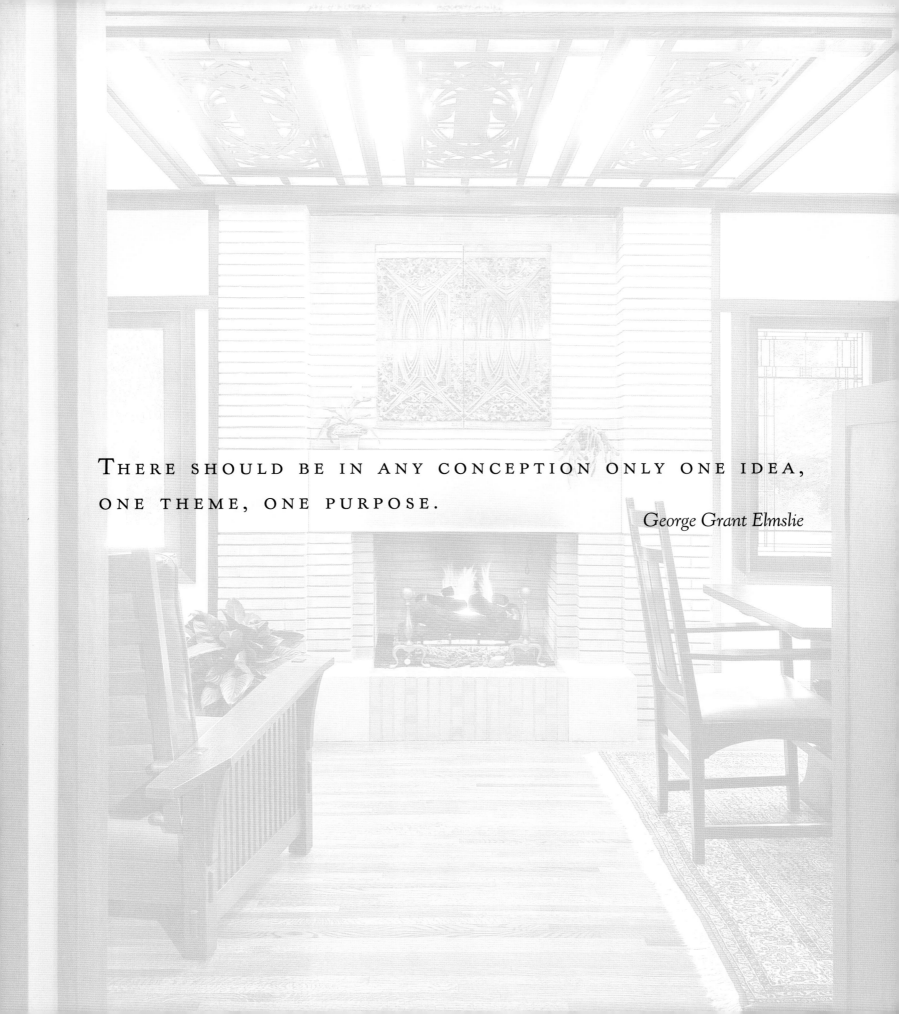

THERE SHOULD BE IN ANY CONCEPTION ONLY ONE IDEA,
ONE THEME, ONE PURPOSE.

George Grant Elmslie

ARCHITECTURE MUST FIRST OF ALL THE ARTS BE OF THE
PEOPLE, BY THE PEOPLE AND FOR THE PEOPLE.

William Gray Purcell

INTRODUCTION

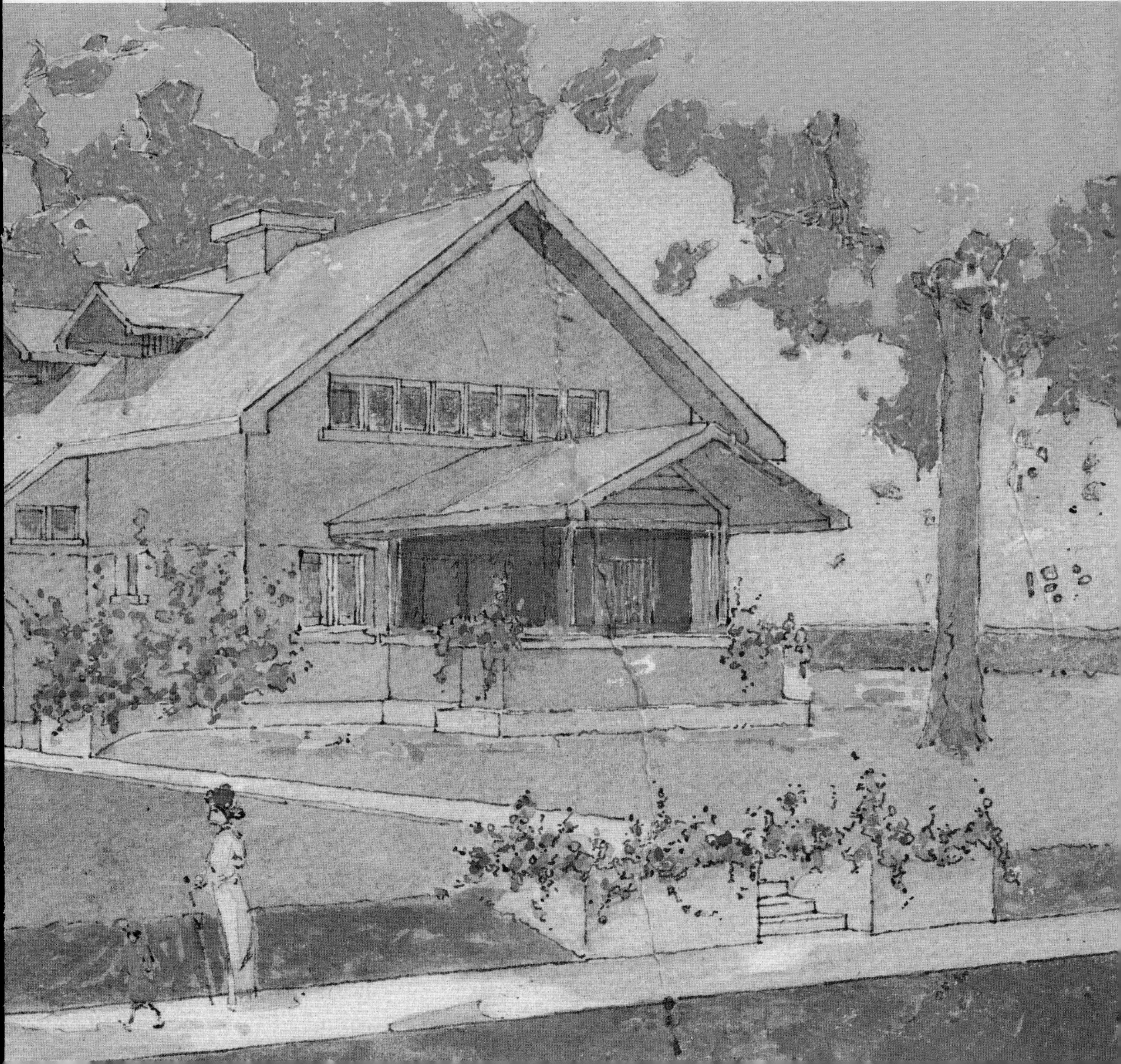

THE PROGRESSIVE SPIRIT

It was an age of optimism in America. An onrush of inventions—automobiles, electric lights, indoor plumbing, and new technology for the home—offered a sense of promise at the dawn of the twentieth century. The Midwest, with its booming economy and progressive ideals, was the perfect stage for a new architecture to suit new times.

William Gray Purcell (1880–1965) and George Grant Elmslie (1869–1952) were two of the era's most visionary architects. Their partnership, forged in Minneapolis in 1910, helped change the direction of home design. Purcell and Elmslie were key players as the drama of a new American architecture first played out in Chicago and then fanned outward to other midwestern cities. Their work—and that of Frank Lloyd Wright, Walter Burley Griffin, George Washington Maher, Barry Byrne, Marion Mahony, William Drummond, John Van Bergen, and a dozen other young architects—became known as the Prairie style.

These architects nurtured on the prairie rejected traditional European styles—Beaux Arts, Queen Anne, Tudor, and other Victorian revivals—in favor of a new American approach to architecture that reflected the landscape, materials, and time of its origin. They emphasized simplicity of design, honest use of natural materials, and respect for the needs of individual clients. Chicago was then the heartland of national housing reform, whose platform called for dignity and a house beautiful for everyone. The clean lines and spacious interiors of the Prairie style suited perfectly.

The innovative Chicago architect Louis H. Sullivan (1856–1924) led the effort to create an authentic American architecture. Imitating historical styles derived from Europe was "unworthy of a free people," he said. A building should unfold organically like a plant from a seed. It should suit its time and place like a river or a tree. Most important, it should flower with ornament. To Sullivan, ornament was not something merely stuck onto the surface as decoration. Instead it flowed logically from the building's form and purpose the way "a certain kind of leaf must appear on a certain kind of tree," he said.

Sullivan was an inspiring figure with an eye for talent. Purcell and Elmslie both learned at his drawing board—Elmslie for two decades. Frank Lloyd Wright (1867–1959), his most well-known protégé, spent about five years soaking up the pronouncements of his "Lieber Meister." Sullivan taught his young draftsmen that an honest architecture based on democratic ideals could elevate the human experience and raise living standards. He applied these precepts to skyscrapers and large commercial buildings such as Chicago's Auditorium Building (1886), noted for its profuse ornament, while his idealistic followers focused on reshaping the American home.

Nature was their greatest inspiration. These designers not only used natural materials and colors but also emphasized the unifying power of nature. Many of the Midwest's progressive architects spent their formative years in the countryside observing nature firsthand. This study and the influence of transcendentalist authors such as Emerson, Thoreau, and Whitman prompted them to look at nature's underlying patterns for ideas on

William Gray Purcell (top) and George Grant Elmslie (above) helped revolutionize residential design at the turn of the twentieth century. They rejected historical revival styles in favor of a progressive new American architecture that expressed the needs of the client and the sweep of the prairie. Based in Minneapolis, their firm turned out all types of buildings but had a special affinity for houses.

CLARK RESIDENCE — CEDAR RAPIDS IOWA   PURCELL-FEICK 8/20/1910

Broad sheltering roofs, bands of casement windows tucked beneath deep eaves, and colors derived from
nature tied the Prairie house to the landscape, as this proposal for the Clark House (1910) in Cedar Rapids,
Iowa, shows. Purcell and Elmslie's fresh approach brought them hundreds of appreciative clients.

how to build and use ornament. The designers also found a kinship with the precepts of the
Arts and Crafts movement and its focus on simplicity and the honest use of natural materials; the Prairie School architects, however, were more captivated by the possibilities of new
technology to improve lives than they were by the movement's handicraft ethic.

The roots of the Prairie style can also be traced to the Progressive political movement at
the turn of the twentieth century, when the Midwest's revolt against the collusion of business interests and government began to have a national impact on social issues. Purcell and
Elmslie in fact considered themselves progressive architects, not Prairie-style architects. But
because their work grew out of the populist sentiments of the midwestern landscape, it
became known as the Prairie style. Houses designed in this style are found far from the
prairie, in places such as Louisiana, Massachusetts, Montana, and Washington. It was not
until 1936 that the movement received a name, when Wright dubbed it the Prairie School to
distinguish it from Sullivan's work, now known as the Chicago School.

Persuading the public to accept new ideas about how they should live was an uphill battle. At the precise moment that Purcell and Elmslie and their colleagues were advocating an indigenous American style, a fascination with classical architecture spurred on by the 1893 World's Columbian Exposition in Chicago was spreading the forms of ancient Greece and Rome across the country. Columns, porticoes, pilasters, and stark classical facades became the norm for banks, churches, libraries, and other public buildings. On the home front, American colonial and picturesque revival styles captured the public's attention.

But on the tree-lined streets of the Midwest, Purcell and Elmslie fought for their own vision, rebelling against the fussy forms imported from Europe. The romance and idealism they brought to their work revealed the best of the progressive American spirit. The firm began in 1907 in Minneapolis as a partnership between Purcell and his college classmate George Feick (1880–1945). Elmslie joined them in 1910 and shortly thereafter Feick, mainly responsible for specifications, departed.

This was the golden era of their practice, when commissions came easily and the designs poured forth in a stunning array. They designed more banks than Sullivan and Wright combined. The largest public Prairie-style building still standing—the Woodbury County Courthouse (1915) in Sioux City, Iowa—is their work. Houses, churches, town halls, bookstores, garages, stables, bandstands, even an open-air theater received their Prairie-style touch. They designed furniture, art glass, lighting, landscaping, stationery, and advertising materials. They contributed articles about progressive architecture to the leading magazines of the day. But it was with their houses, the subject of this book, that the firm's talents really soared. Some of the most extraordinary houses in the Midwest came from Purcell and Elmslie's office.

They had only a few short years to work together. World War I ended the nation's building boom as well as the romantic notion of an indigenous American style. Both had personal setbacks that changed their lives. The firm officially dissolved in 1921. But the revolution in home design they began is still felt today, as homeowners and builders look to earlier eras for inspiration. The simple elegance and honest, nature-based designs they fostered are as timeless today as they were a century ago.

The Prairie house's cruciform plan maximized living space. The dining room of the Steven House (1909) in Eau Claire, Wisconsin, is secluded in its own wing (opposite). Innate pattern comes from the oak bands that crisscross the walls and ceiling. A new oak dining set was made by Amish woodworkers.

Purcell and Elmslie grouped art glass windows to increase their impact. In the Wiethoff House (1917) in Minneapolis, a pair of windows with a linear tulip design makes a pleasing impression as they frame the view.

COMMON BOND

William Gray Purcell and George Grant Elmslie were the most productive of all the Prairie School partnerships. With Purcell's business and family connections, personal charm, and analytical approach and Elmslie's extraordinary artistry and design ability, they eclipsed even Frank Lloyd Wright—who retreated to Europe for a time—as the leaders of the progressive Prairie style between 1910 and 1921. Raised in an atmosphere of wealth and privilege, Purcell was handsome and intelligent with a flair for public relations. The Scottish-born Elmslie was shy and unassuming and came from a large family of humble means. Although their temperaments and backgrounds were radically different, Purcell and Elmslie shared a common bond: the intense zeal for creating an original American architecture.

All the elements of a cozy winter evening are evident in the living room of the Minneapolis home that Purcell designed for his wife, Edna, and two sons in 1913. The family often shared informal meals on the raised hearth before a roaring fire. The experience was heightened by iridescent glass shimmering in the fireplace's mortar joints and the joyful dance of blue herons in the mural by Charles Livingston Bull.

George Grant Elmslie

Elmslie was born in 1869 (some sources say 1871) on a farm called Foot O'Hill in the Aberdeen Highlands of northern Scotland. Years later he still recalled the bucolic landscape that held his imagination. "I used to play . . . in a beautiful country, with winding streams and aged forest—rich and fragrant valleys—and old, old hills covered with white and purple heather." Elmslie's father, John, was a weaver by trade who turned to farming to support his family of ten. When he found it impossible to eke out a living on his small farm, the family immigrated to America in 1884, where John found a managerial job in a Chicago meatpacking plant.

George showed early promise as an artist and at his parents' suggestion apprenticed to become an architect. "It was my parents' desire," he later wrote, "that I pursue a professional life as an engineer and architect—somehow." In 1887 he took a job as a draftsman for the Chicago architect Joseph Lyman Silsbee, a champion of the rustic Shingle style inspired by New England's past. He was in good company. Young Frank Lloyd Wright and George Washington Maher, future pioneers of the Prairie School movement, were also employed by Silsbee. Elmslie and Wright soon struck up a friendship. When the ever-ambitious Wright moved to the office of Adler and Sullivan in 1888—one of the most prestigious firms in Chicago—he arranged for Elmslie to join him the next year. This would be the beginning of a two-decade relationship in which Elmslie rose from draftsman to virtual partner of Sullivan's. He never attained the title of partner, but he became indispensable to Sullivan: critiquing his essays and handling clients and business matters, in addition to working on designs.

The timid Elmslie blossomed at the drafting table, quickly learning to master and even surpass Sullivan's elegant nature-based ornament. He was devoted to Sullivan and his idealistic vision of an authentic American architecture. Yet Sullivan could be difficult. His rigid personality and volatile temper eventually doomed his practice and ruined his partnership with Dankmar Adler. Wright left after a few years in a dispute over his moonlighting. But Elmslie stayed through it all. When his contemporaries were presiding over their own practices, he stood loyally by as Sullivan's chief draftsman, playing a silent yet major role in many of Sullivan's designs.

"Beginning in 1895 and until 1909 I did 99⅗ percent of [Sullivan's design work]," Elmslie wrote years later to Purcell. "When I left some knowing people wondered what had happened to Sullivan's ornament." Much of the ornament, labeled "Sullivanesque" by historians, was actually designed by Elmslie. The intricate cast-iron filigree on the Schlesinger and Mayer (Carson Pirie Scott) store (1899–1904) in Chicago and nearly all the terra-cotta and art glass ornament of the National Farmers' Bank (1906) in Owatonna, Minnesota, are from Elmslie's hand. Elmslie claimed to have created "more different motifs than [Sullivan] ever dreamed of."

In 1903 Elmslie attended a dinner party that would change his life. There he met Purcell, a decade younger, and the two embarked on a lengthy discussion of the merits of an organic, indigenous architecture. Despite the age difference they became great friends, and Elmslie secured a short apprenticeship for Purcell with Sullivan. Although it lasted only five months, Purcell and Elmslie remained in close contact, even after Purcell established his own firm in Minneapolis. Purcell repeatedly asked Elmslie to join his practice, but Elmslie refused to leave Sullivan despite a drastic downturn in business.

Elmslie was the master of ornament, surpassing Wright and even Sullivan with his lush, organic designs. When he joined Purcell and Feick, the results were dazzling. In the Powers House (1910) in Minneapolis, the dining room buffet carries one of his signature perforated-wood motifs and a delicate ring of stencils floats above.

Elmslie married late in life and was devoted to his beloved Bonnie. Unlike Purcell, who designed several family homes, Elmslie never created a house for Bonnie or himself. After their marriage in 1910, they moved into an apartment building where William and Edna Purcell were already living.

By early 1909 Sullivan's commissions had nearly dried up and Elmslie was on half salary, yet he stayed on. He always believed that he would inherit Sullivan's practice, but by the end of the year Sullivan's fortunes declined to such an extent that there was no practice to inherit. And with no money to pay even half a salary, Elmslie was forced to leave. "The wrench is terrible," Elmslie confided to Purcell. After twenty years of loyal service, he was out of a job for the first time in his life. Nearing forty and never having risen formally above the status of chief draftsman, he had to start over.

In early 1910 he finally accepted Purcell's offer to join his Minneapolis firm, and, after years of bachelorhood, Elmslie fell in love. He displayed the same shyness and self-doubt in courtship as he had in other relationships. "I do hesitate to bother her with my presence," he wrote Purcell. "I am so much of an antiquity." On September 14, 1910, Elmslie married a twenty-seven-year-old Scottish lass named Bonnie Marie Hunter in Chicago. Shortly thereafter, they moved to an apartment in Minneapolis. The insecurity he had experienced for so long seemed to vanish. He was doing the work he loved with Bonnie by his side. Emslie was about to embark on the happiest period of his life.

William Gray Purcell

Purcell was just nine years old when Frank Lloyd Wright began to build his home and studio a few doors away from the house of Purcell's parents in Oak Park, Illinois. "I had never seen anything remotely resembling it," he said of seeing a sketch of the house. But it was the modern work of Louis Sullivan that most captured his imagination. A trip to Sullivan's Auditorium Building in Chicago with his grandmother when he was ten years old persuaded him to become an architect. He was so impressed by Sullivan's colorful Transportation Building, the only progressive design on display at the World's Columbian Exposition of 1893, that he visited the fair fifty-four times.

Born on July 2, 1880, in the Chicago suburb of Wilmette, he spent most of his childhood with his maternal grandparents in their home in Oak Park. His father, Charles, was a wealthy grain merchant and a member of the Chicago board of trade. His mother, Anna Catherine Gray Purcell, was the daughter of William Cunningham Gray, publisher and editor of *The Interior,* a progressive Presbyterian magazine, and Catherine Garns Gray, an artist. His grandparents' home, where he chose to live after an apparent dispute between his mother and grandmother, was filled with books, music, art, and progressive ideas. "There was always much good reading aloud, reading of poetry," Purcell said. "The *Atlantic Monthly* on the table always. . . ."

Purcell's summers were spent with family and friends in an isolated retreat deep in the north Wisconsin woods, where his grandfather had re-created the rustic Ohio homestead of his childhood. At Island Lake, as the compound was called, Purcell developed the love of nature shared by all the Prairie architects. "These years . . . coming to know life in the primitive

The architects and their wives gather for a meal about 1910 with Catherine Gray, Purcell's grandmother, in the Minneapolis house that he designed for her in 1907 (below left). Purcell sits at the head of the table, with George Feick and Edna Purcell on the left and George Elmslie and Bonnie Hunter on the right. The tented ceiling became a trademark of the firm's residential designs. William and Edna Purcell and their two adopted sons, James and Douglas, pose for a photograph around 1916 in the living room of their Minneapolis home (below right). The family lived in the house for only a few years. It was sold in 1919 to Anson and Edna Cutts and is now known as the Purcell-Cutts House, a property of the Minneapolis Institute of Arts.

  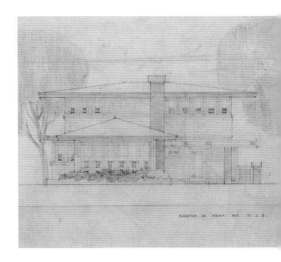

Purcell's enthusiasm for new ways of designing found form in the 1907 house he shared with his grand-mother until late 1908 (above left). Corner casement windows, a low hipped roof, and a simplified but sturdy design introduced his new architecture firm to Minneapolis. Purcell's career received a boost in 1909 when his father, Charles Purcell, commissioned a house in River Forest, Illinois (above center). Purcell used the opportunity to showcase his "joy of color," discovered on a sojourn to Europe with George Feick in 1906. He later painted over a photograph of the house, trying to re-create the original hues of the stucco and red brick walls and slate blue roof after subsequent owners had changed it. By the time Purcell produced a home for his family in 1913 (above right), his ideas about progressive design had reached maturity. Created in collaboration with Elmslie, it was, Purcell said, "a brilliantly successful project in every way."

forest, in very simple cabins without 'conveniences,' really shaped my life, ruled my ideals and ambitions. I came to . . . value the goodness of plain 'uneducated' people and accept demo-cratic relations with all men as the normal way of life."

Purcell attended the College of Architecture at Cornell University in Ithaca, New York, but his views on architecture soon collided with the classically oriented Beaux-Arts curriculum. He graduated in 1903 and returned home to Oak Park and considered appren-ticing to Wright, but his father disapproved of the flamboyant architect's lifestyle. Instead, Purcell secured work with the local Prairie architect E. E. Roberts and later with his idol, Louis Sullivan, through Elmslie. His experience under the tutelage of Sullivan and Elmslie proved critical to his development as an architect. Purcell and Elmslie established a close personal and professional relationship that would blossom when the two became full partners.

After a two-year stint apprenticing with architects in San Francisco and Seattle, Purcell decided on a year-long grand tour of Europe in 1906. Accompanied by his college classmate George Feick, he traveled to Italy, Turkey, and Greece, observing classical architecture, as well as to Scandinavia and the Netherlands, where he met with the progressive architect H. P. Berlage. Filled with enthusiasm, Purcell decided to start his own firm offering progressive architecture. Feick, trained as an engineer, persuaded him that Minneapolis was fertile ground with less competition than Chicago.

Purcell would build two houses in Minneapolis to showcase the firm's talents, one for his grandmother, Catherine Gray, the other for his wife, Edna Summy, a Wellesley graduate. The couple had married on December 29, 1908. They lived for a while with Purcell's grand-mother, later moving into an apartment. In 1911 they adopted their first son, James, and began to think of building a home. That house, named for Edna Purcell, fulfilled Purcell's ideal of the progressive home.

William Gray Purcell, seated at center, confers with his partner George Grant Elmslie, standing, in the summer of 1910, while George Feick concentrates at his desk in the new firm's well-lighted office (above left). Drawings for some of their projects hang from picture rails. Purcell, Feick and Elmslie's office was run like a democracy. Ideas from any member of "the team," as Purcell called the changing group of draftsmen and artists, were respected. "The line-up of the team was not from top to bottom but hand in hand," he wrote. And all members "believed that they were really contributing something unique and characteristic to American life." In their office around 1911 (above right), from the left are George Feick, the draftswoman Marion Alice Parker, a man named Ireland, George Grant Elmslie, and the draftsman Paul Haugen.

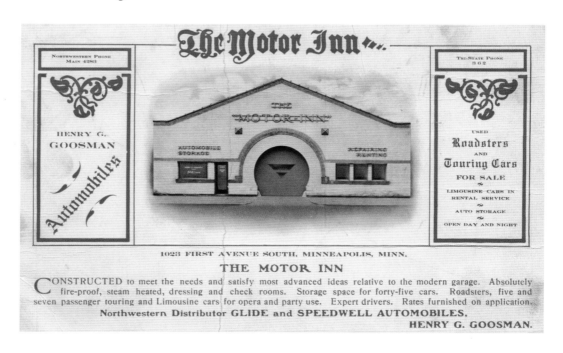

PRAIRIE HOME COMPANIONS

Years after William Purcell took the northbound train from Chicago to Minneapolis in 1907 to meet George Feick, he movingly described that trip: "It was twenty below zero in Minnesota. The thin lemon sunlight, as tight as frozen sailcloth, slatted past the soft flowing sleeping cars. Through the triple glazed Pullman windows could be seen the clustered dusty tubes of grain elevators." When he arrived the two men rented rooms in a boarding house, set up their architecture practice on the tenth floor of the New York Life Building (with financial assistance from Purcell's father), and wondered how they were going to drum up work in a strange city where they knew only one other person and the phone book listed two dozen well-established architecture offices.

Commissions came slowly for the fledgling firm. They had no examples to show prospective clients, and it was a struggle to educate them about contemporary design. Gradually, however, Purcell's family connections opened doors in small midwestern towns. The Minneapolis house that Purcell designed for his grandmother, helped by advice from George Elmslie, showcased his architectural ideas. With its innovative use of an asymmetrical entry, tented ceilings, an open floor plan, a raised hearth, and casement windows, this 1907 house forecast the firm's commitment to modern, livable spaces.

By the time Elmslie joined Purcell in early 1910, the firm had recorded dozens of commissions: churches, a sanitarium, a college building, a warehouse, a bank, a Motor Inn (the first building to service automobiles in Minneapolis), and about twenty houses and residential alterations. Many of these remained only plans on paper, but Purcell and Feick were rapidly gaining a reputation for high-quality, practical designs. With a cruciform plan that influenced their later work, the Steven House (1909) in Eau Claire, Wisconsin, illustrated the firm's new thinking. The Stewart Memorial Church (1909) in Minneapolis—notable for its radical flat roof, intimate seating area, and tall windows—demonstrated their ability to apply progressive ideas in an ecclesiastical setting.

The firm's prosperity did not go unnoticed. Just before he left for a two-year sojourn in Europe in late 1909, Frank Lloyd Wright asked Purcell to take over his Oak Park practice while he was away. Accepting Wright's proposal would have dramatically increased business, but Purcell, after consulting with Elmslie, turned Wright down. Never recording the real reason, he wrote in 1949 that "many factors finally determined the partners to forgo this seemingly attractive offer." Wright tried other architects without success and eventually left his work in the hands of a non-Prairie School designer, Hermann von Holst.

With work picking up, Purcell and Feick gathered around them a group of draftsmen, artists, and designers to help out in the busy office. Purcell christened them "the team" and willingly shared credit with each member. "There were no important differentials of class or station, no priorities of talent," Purcell said. "The good idea—the resolution of a tough problem—could come from anyone in the office or on the job." Heralding their progressive thinking in matters other than architecture, the first full-time draftsperson was a woman, Marion Alice Parker.

"Storage space for forty-five cars" proclaims an advertisement featuring a colorful rendering of the modern Motor Inn the firm of Purcell and Feick designed in 1907 for Henry Goosman—the first structure in Minneapolis built to service automobiles (opposite). It also sold and rented vehicles. "Roadsters, five and seven passenger touring and Limousine cars for opera and party use," boasts the ad.

Elmslie's addition to the firm, which was renamed Purcell, Feick and Elmslie, brought about an immediate change as their architecture evolved from the exacting, self-disciplined designs of Purcell to embrace Elmslie's exuberant, daring, and highly ornamented compositions. The pair worked in unison: Elmslie, the artist, churned out glorious ornament and complex architecture designs. Purcell, the analyst with a talent for public relations, secured commissions and managed the office, all the while developing designs. Feick, trained as an engineer, dealt with specifications. After meeting with a client, Purcell would generally prepare a sketch that became the starting point of the design. Elmslie would add his thoughts, sometimes maintaining Purcell's basic concept, at other times developing a new solution. Once a final design was reached, the sketches were turned over to the office draftsmen. Their collaboration, said Elmslie, was of such a "frank and intimate nature" that it was "osmotic in a sense."

When Elmslie was occupied with other work, Purcell would occasionally develop a complete design, often with assistance from Marion Parker. After reviewing Purcell's plan, Elmslie added ornament or other features. For the Adair House of 1913 in Owatonna, Minnesota, for example, Purcell worked out the house design with Parker; Elmslie later composed designs for art glass, sawn-wood ornament, light fixtures, and an arched fireplace. Both thus contributed substantially to the design process. As Purcell noted, "In this team if you look for one partner as aesthete and the other as executive, the usual 'designer'-businessman, artist-engineer combination[,] you won't find it."

As the firm pursued its vision of a new American architecture, residential clients came pouring in. Purcell and Elmslie's first large residential collaboration, the Powers House of 1910 in Minneapolis, sealed their reputation for producing elegant groundbreaking designs. Former patrons of Louis Sullivan—including Charles R. Crane; his daughter, Josephine Crane Bradley; Carl K. Bennett; and Henry Babson—steered new commissions their way. Middle-class clients such as Henry Goosman, Maurice Wolf, and Charles Parker also received remarkable designs celebrating the firm's commitment to comfort and beauty for everyone. Individually designed lighting, built-in furnishings, art glass, and other ornament made these homes complete statements of progressive twentieth-century design.

Bank commissions were prized among architects of the period because their prominence, usually on Main Street, offered an excellent showcase for attracting new clients. With

Elmslie's creative input, the firm landed several important bank commissions, including the Exchange Bank in Grand Meadow, Minnesota, and the First National Bank in Rhinelander, Wisconsin, both designed in 1910 and testifying to Elmslie's influence on Purcell. "One can see in our Exchange Bank . . . the new brightness which George G. Elmslie put into my solemn syllogisms," Purcell wrote. Other bank designs would follow, including the crowning jewel, the Merchants National Bank (1912) in Winona, Minnesota, with its vast skylight, shimmering walls of art glass, and functional modern interior.

In their zeal to shape every aspect of design, the firm also created stationery, business cards, signage, and even advertising campaigns for their commercial clients. For the 1912 Edison Shop in Chicago, their design focused on how to increase sales, a first for an architecture firm, Purcell claimed. "Up to this time, the business problems, of advertising, selling, sales psychology, consumer reaction, concern with 'package[,]' dramatization of product, employee deportment, had simply not been touched by the architect," Purcell wrote.

With work increasing, additional draftsmen and artists made significant contributions. Draftsmen Lawrence Fournier, Lawrence Clapp, Frederick Strauel, John A. Walquist, Emil Frank, and Leroy A. Gaarder transformed Purcell and Elmslie's sketches into working drawings. Outside the office, the terra-cotta modeler Kristian Schneider of the American Terra Cotta Company, glassmaker Edward L. Sharretts, silversmith Robert Jarvie, cabinetmakers Gustav Weber and Ralph Pelton, and furniture manufacturers John S. Bradstreet and George Mann Niedecken brought the partners' imaginings to life.

Harold and Josephine Crane Bradley were devoted clients who commissioned several designs from the firm, including a sophisticated new home in Madison, Wisconsin, in 1914 to replace their four-year-old Louis Sullivan house, which had been a wedding present from Josephine's father, the industrialist Charles R. Crane. The spacious new residence in Madison (opposite and below) cost about $35,000 to build.

In 1912, as the firm was approaching the zenith of its creativity, Elmslie's wife of just two years died following a surgical procedure. He was devastated and never recovered from the loss. Despite Purcell's protestations, Elmslie moved back to Chicago to live with his sisters. Purcell and Elmslie maintained their partnership, with Elmslie operating from an office in Chicago, four hundred miles away. Feick, never as enthusiastic as his partners about progressive design, left the firm in early 1913.

Even with the great distance between them, Purcell and Elmslie soon had a more productive and varied practice than Wright's. While Wright's work had been almost exclusively residential, Purcell and Elmslie designed churches, town halls, fire stations, schools, offices, factories, banks, and landscaping, although houses were the backbone of their practice. Enthusiastic clients would often help them find other commissions or sign up for more than one building. With Wright's departure for Europe and the gifted Walter Burley Griffin and Marion Mahony working in Australia, Purcell and Elmslie became the Prairie School's primary designers.

Purcell continued to press for the cause of an indigenous American architecture by accepting speaking engagements and writing articles, often in collaboration with Elmslie. *Western Architect,* published in Minneapolis, was one of the few architecture journals to feature the kind of architecture they favored. In 1913 it devoted an entire issue to Purcell and Elmslie's work. Two more full issues came in 1915, the same year the firm received its most significant commission, the Woodbury County Courthouse in Sioux City, Iowa. Designed in collaboration with William L. Steele, a local architect who once worked with Elmslie in Sullivan's office, the building is filled with lavish terra-cotta ornament and exquisite murals. It remains the largest Prairie-style civic structure ever built.

Just as Purcell and Elmslie were enjoying their most productive years, the cause of progressive architecture suddenly lost steam. By 1916, at the height of World War I, the zeal for this new American style took a back seat to a burgeoning interest in imported historical styles. To keep their struggling business in operation, Purcell sold his property in Minneapolis and moved his family to Pennsylvania in 1917 to take a job as advertising manager for Charles O. Alexander's industrial leather belting company. Purcell's original plan included operating a branch office there while Elmslie ran the offices in Chicago and Minneapolis, where they maintained a small staff. The firm designed two factory buildings and remodeled an office for the Alexander brothers, but few other commissions came along.

Purcell remained in this position for three years until a dispute with Alexander prompted him to leave. In 1919 he relocated to Portland, Oregon, to join his cousin Charles Purcell's bridge-building business although he ended up continuing to practice architecture; Elmslie kept the office going in Chicago. But by 1921 it was no longer economically feasible to continue, and Purcell dissolved the practice. This was a huge blow to Elmslie, but the two eventually resolved their differences. Each continued to practice architecture on his own.

Elmslie remained faithful to the forms of the progressive style, designing several college buildings and other structures in the Midwest with more restrained ornament. He lived with his sisters for the rest of his life, wrote a few articles on architecture, and took on the job of dealing with Sullivan's archives after his death in 1924. Elmslie and Wright were often at odds

Banks were a Purcell and Elmslie specialty. The Merchants National Bank (1912) in Winona, Minnesota, is one of their finest because of its sumptuous ornament (left). A terra-cotta eagle—a symbol of strength—is set into a bold arch above the entrance. Walls of shimmering art glass bathe the interior in natural light.

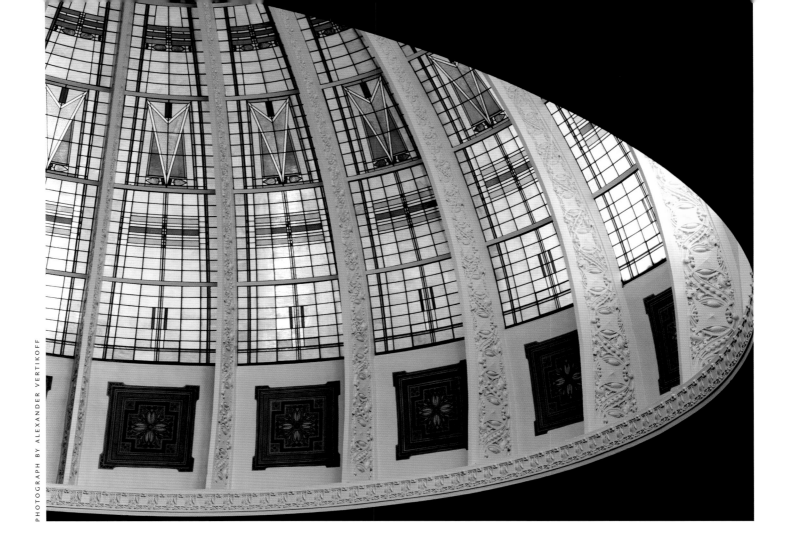

PHOTOGRAPH BY ALEXANDER VERTIKOFF

Purcell and Elmslie's vision of a new American architecture extended to every building type, including the stunning Woodbury County Courthouse (1915) in Sioux City, Iowa. Designed in collaboration with the local architect William L. Steele, it is the largest Prairie-style public building to be constructed. Elmslie's deft hand with ornament is evident in the soaring art glass dome hovering over the central rotunda.

over who was the true standard bearer of the Sullivan legacy. Elmslie died in 1952 at the age of eighty-three.

Purcell continued to practice, working with his former draftsman Frederick Strauel, who maintained an office in Minneapolis. In 1931 Purcell was diagnosed with tuberculosis and entered a sanitarium in Banning, California. Shortly thereafter, his adopted son Douglas died of meningitis, and he and Edna divorced. From the 1930s to the 1950s, Purcell recorded his thoughts on the firm's work in a series of autobiographical essays he called "Parabiographies." He lived to see Purcell and Elmslie's designs celebrated in 1953 in a major retrospective at the Walker Art Center in Minneapolis. He died in 1965 at the age of eighty-five.

In their few years together, Purcell and Elmslie created some of America's finest architecture. They produced hundreds of successful designs in twenty-two states. Neither of them could have done it alone. Purcell's proclivity for public relations and shrewd analysis brought in the clients and provoked new solutions. Elmslie's artistic gifts and vast experience took their work to new heights. As Purcell recalled later in life, "Purcell and Elmslie were part of a team. Each could do something the other could not.... They were friends and brothers, a deep bond continuing to this day." Together they exalted natural materials, championed open house plans, shaped buildings to the land, and planted the seeds of an indigenous American architecture.

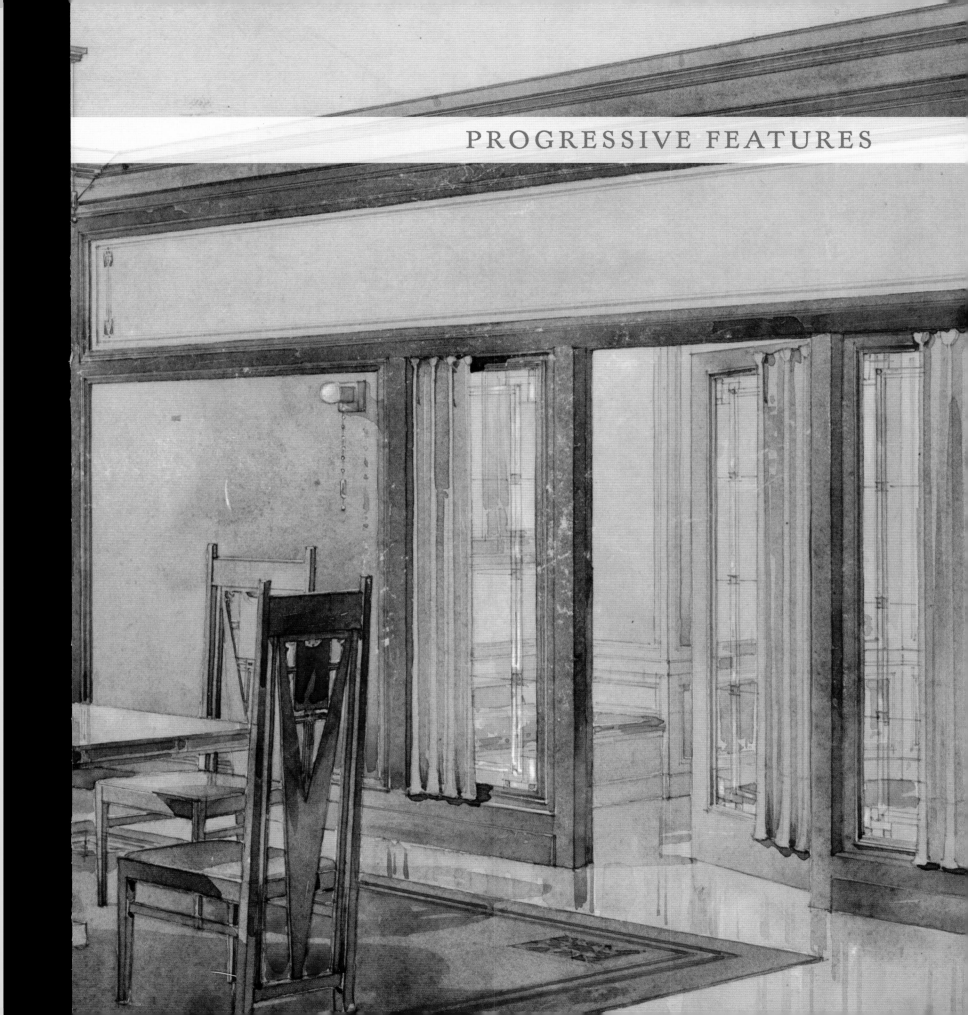

A New House on the Prairie

Throughout the midwestern prairie, in towns with names such as Red Wing, Minnesota, and Eau Claire, Wisconsin, extraordinary early-twentieth-century houses fit snugly into the landscape. Crafted from natural materials with free-flowing interiors and grand sweeps of art glass in radiant hues, these homes are paragons of the Prairie style, a new way of building that took the Midwest by storm a century ago.

Working together from 1910 to 1921, Purcell and Elmslie built more than sixty Prairie-style houses in twelve states and designed dozens more. Most were built in the Midwest—in Minnesota, Wisconsin, and Illinois—yet Purcell and Elmslie also brought their form of progressive architecture to the East and West Coasts in buildings constructed in Massachusetts, Pennsylvania, Montana, California, and Oregon.

Their houses are undeniably American, tied to the land by local materials and low, spreading forms. Each was created for a specific place, client, and use—signature elements of the Prairie style. It took vision and courage for their clients to build a new type of house amid the Victorian confections and Mediterranean palazzos of the day. Yet these thrillingly modern houses found champions not only in larger cities but also in the smallest towns.

Purcell and Elmslie enthusiastically took up the cause of creating a new house for the modern American family. They advocated both a new way of building and a new way of living—a rejection of stuffy Victorian parlors for clean lines, spacious interiors, and unlimited possibilities. "Houses should not be clamps to force us to the same things three hundred and sixty-five days in the year . . . but they should be backgrounds for expressing ourselves in three hundred and sixty-five different ways if we are natural enough to do so," Purcell proselytized.

The firm's houses are most noted for their sumptuous integrated ornament, but the architects were innovative in other ways: their fidelity to open plans, their use of rich color, their ideas for furniture design and kitchen efficiency, and their overall approach to human comfort. They took everything into account: "The outside, inside, and structure of the finished product always affectionately related to earth, to people, to sky, rain, sun, wind, and to the future," enumerated Purcell.

Ornament was more than mere decoration for Purcell and Elmslie. It expressed the building's inner spirit, as Louis Sullivan had taught, so it was essential to the design. Elmslie was the master of ornament. His distinctive palette is immediately identifiable, particularly his fondness for diamonds, V shapes, convex and concave geometric forms, combinations of circles and squares, and plantlike organic shapes. Themes and variations of these motifs appear in art glass, stencils, sawn wood, terra cotta, furnishings, lighting, and textiles, all of them unifying the design like notes in a symphony.

Purcell and Elmslie gave the Adair House (1913) in Owatonna, Minnesota, a feeling of oriental simplicity (opposite). Built-in cabinets with clean, simple lines freed up floor space, making the house feel larger and less cluttered. More freedom was achieved with generous doorways that allowed rooms to flow effortlessly into one another. Woodwork, door frames, and cabinets in the same materials and finishes harmonized the design.

Purcell worried that "the decorative aspect of their work" might overshadow "the more important and significant factors of their basic principles." Among these was inventive use of open floor plans. Purcell and Elmslie looked to Frank Lloyd Wright for ideas on breaking out of confining boxlike rooms, and then they found their own voice in a concept that made small houses feel larger. Like Wright, they moved the fireplace from its traditional location on the outside wall to the center of the house, allowing the living and dining areas to flow as one space around the hearth. They also grouped windows on the common outer wall for maximum effect, flooding both rooms with daylight.

Another distinguishing feature is the use of brilliant color, far beyond the nature-based shades most associated with the Prairie style: deep reds, bright blues, salmon pinks, and rich greens. Purcell claimed that they were "among the first American architects to make bold use of color in all their buildings." This was a legacy from Louis Sullivan, who also favored rich, deep colors, and from Purcell's travels in Europe. Accents of bright hues on sawn wood, stencils, textiles, and enameled terra cotta called attention to decorative features and helped harmonize the design. Exterior stucco was not white or off-white, as so many houses are today, but instead a sandy salmon color that blended into rather than contrasted with the dark wood trim.

Although most of the firm's residences feature the low hipped roof that gives the Prairie-style house its earth-bound form, Purcell admitted a lifelong fondness for high pitched roofs. He liked the "aspirational quality," he said, the way a tall top hat of a roof might imbue a house with an intrinsic sense of shelter. Where Wright eliminated the attic to give his houses a horizontal silhouette, Purcell raised the roofline high, particularly in the Heitman House (1916) in Helena, Montana, with its ninety-degree pitch. Yet when he built his own home (1913) in Minneapolis, Purcell chose a flat roof, perhaps as a showpiece for attracting progressive clients.

The needs of the housewife were also of primary importance, particularly for Purcell, who made a study of kitchen design. The average woman of the day lived in a house designed in the "gay nineties," Purcell said, which was "gay enough" if they were fortunate to afford a maid. These "wife killers," he noted, had large rooms with high ceilings and many stairs, making them a chore to keep clean. Purcell studied ways to make kitchens labor saving and streamlined. He put the ice box closer to the work space to eliminate steps. He lowered sink heights and included "newfangled" items such as kitchen cupboards and breakfast nooks. "My kitchens were long in advance of their time," he claimed.

Purcell and Elmslie also analyzed traffic patterns to determine the best place to put windows, doors, and even light switches. They studied the human form to determine how to make furniture comfortable, functional, and beautiful. They added sun porches and sleeping porches—sometimes more than one to a floor—for healthy living and included radiators for year-round use. And they were among the first to incorporate a garage into a house's design.

Purcell and Elmslie's attention to both the spiritual and the physical needs of clients make their houses works of art as well as wonderful places to raise families and entertain friends. As Purcell said, "Architecture must first of all the arts be of the people, by the people and for the people."

The fireplace took up its role as the heart of the house when Purcell and Elmslie moved it from its traditional place on the outside wall. They also gave it a high mantel and a raised hearth for a modern, new look. Natural wicker furniture suited the progressive Atkinson House (1910) in Bismarck, North Dakota, meeting budgets that did not allow custom designs. Sturdy Stickley and Mission furnishings also fit in well.

FREE AND OPEN PLANS

Purcell and Elmslie helped reshape the American home to suit modern times and modern lifestyles by remaking interior spaces. They rejected cramped Victorian rooms filled with clutter in favor of spacious rooms with wide openings, furnishings with simple lines, and grouped windows that could drink in the natural light. They eliminated walls whenever possible and treated the lower floor as one large space. "The wall began to give up its burden to play a happier role," Purcell explained, following the lead of Frank Lloyd Wright.

Open floor plans made even small houses seem larger and united family members in less formal spaces. Instead of cloistered parlors and other specialized rooms, living areas became spacious and multipurpose, zoned for various activities: a writing table tucked into a corner, a cozy inglenook with built-in benches next to the fireplace, or a window seat to view nature gave each family member a quiet and beautiful corner in which to relax.

Rooms were defined not by walls but by various levels, built-in cabinets, or the location of the fireplace. A common floor plan called for the dining room and living room to flow as one around a central hearth. Sometimes a cabinet was built into one end of the fireplace, creating an L-shaped partial wall; at eye level, it screened dining and living rooms but did not visually close off the space. Variations of this plan—always personalized to fit the individual client—are found in many of the firm's small and medium-sized houses, such as the Goosman, Beebe, Wiethoff, and Owre residences in Minneapolis and St. Paul. To add to the sense of spaciousness, the living room often opened directly onto a glassed-in veranda to draw in the outside and create additional three-season living space.

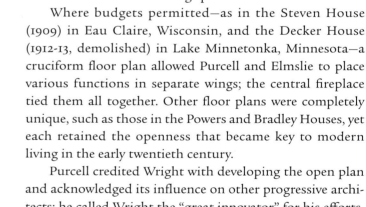

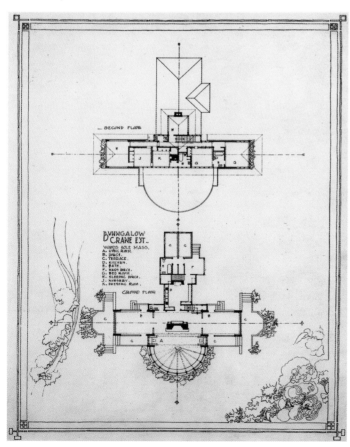

Where budgets permitted—as in the Steven House (1909) in Eau Claire, Wisconsin, and the Decker House (1912-13, demolished) in Lake Minnetonka, Minnesota—a cruciform floor plan allowed Purcell and Elmslie to place various functions in separate wings; the central fireplace tied them all together. Other floor plans were completely unique, such as those in the Powers and Bradley Houses, yet each retained the openness that became key to modern living in the early twentieth century.

Purcell credited Wright with developing the open plan and acknowledged its influence on other progressive architects; he called Wright the "great innovator" for his efforts. Yet each of these contemporaries brought his or her own vision to this pioneering way of living. Nowhere is this more apparent than in Purcell's own 1913 Minneapolis home, the firm's greatest ode to the open plan. Space within the Purcell-Cutts House, as it is known today, is manipulated both horizontally and vertically to create an astonishing sense of freedom for its time. Useless divisions were eliminated. "A new place appeared within the house," Purcell announced, "all free and open."

The elimination of unnecessary walls opened views from one end of a house to the other. Living and dining rooms in the Owre House (1911) in Minneapolis flow seamlessly around the central hearth (above). Natural light spills out from a shared bank of casement windows. Ribbons of wood trim tie everything together.

Purcell and Elmslie turned to a cruciform plan to liberate space within the Bradley summer bungalow (1911) on the Crane estate in Woods Hole, Massachusetts (opposite). Armlike wings cloaked in glass reach out from the central fireplace on the first floor, with few solid walls to impede the flow of space. A curved prow with windows all around juts out from the house to take in the spectacular ocean views.

FIRE-LOVING HEARTHS

Fireplaces held a sacred place in the hearts of Purcell and Elmslie. Personal experiences shaped their view of the hearth as a powerful symbol of home and family. "Fireplaces! You ought to have seen our kitchen fireplace in Scotland," Elmslie fondly recalled of his childhood. It was "about ten feet wide and four feet deep.... We burned peat mostly and what heat from it.... Kitchen was the living room, too, everybody in the family was there."

Purcell's own affection for a warming fire was formed during summers spent with his grandparents and their friends in the Wisconsin woods, sharing conversation and compan-

ionship around a campfire. But it was his tour of Europe with George Feick in 1906 that introduced the notion of a raised hearth, a central feature in the firm's designs beginning in 1907 with the home for Catherine Gray, Purcell's grandmother. "In this house we developed the very first raised hearth fireplace, suggested by the very open kitchen working fires at low table height . . . seen in Swedish folk farm houses in 1906. . . . In constant use in our fire-loving family, we found it just right—a joyful picture within the very substance of the room wall."

Like a primordial fire deep within a sheltering cave, the fireplaces in nearly all Purcell

and Elmslie homes were situated in the central core of the house instead of on the more traditional outside wall. The extra structural support provided by the fireplace allowed them to eliminate unnecessary walls and freed up floor space. Often a veranda was situated just off the living room, with French doors opening wide for a direct view of the fireplace; there one could enjoy the comfort of a warming fire while encircled in nature. This ability to convey both the openness of nature and the intimacy of a protective fire was one of the architects' greatest achievements.

To underscore the hearth's importance, Purcell and Elmslie often incorporated lavish decoration or intimate inglenooks into their designs. Murals depicting pastoral landscapes in the Purcell-Cutts and Charles Purcell Houses drew on the force of nature to showcase the hearth. The Powers House fireplace is adorned with sumptuous terra cotta in flowing organic forms and is framed by not one but two inglenooks. The Adair House in Owatonna and the Hoyt House in Red Wing both feature sparkling glass mosaics.

The idea of a raised hearth was not always an easy sell. For the Sexton House (1910) in Lake Minnetonka, Minnesota, Purcell and Elmslie designed raised hearths for the living room and the den. "But not for Mrs. Sexton! 'Out' they were to come, and incensed she was about our even proposing them," Purcell recalled. "But Sexton liked the idea—said anyway the den was his, he wanted a place to put his feet up." So he got his wish in his den. A month later, Purcell and Elmslie received a call from an embarrassed Mrs. Sexton. "Could we rebuild the living room fireplace to make a raised hearth as we had planned? Everybody liked the den best and no one wanted to use the living room." Sadly, it was too expensive to change.

Deep inside the Powers House (1910) in Minneapolis, a lavish terra-cotta frieze crowns the austere gray brick fireplace with a burst of color (left). Two built-in benches embrace this masterpiece of ornament, the room's focal point. The hearth is raised, as Purcell and Elmslie liked.

POETIC ORNAMENT

For Purcell and Elmslie ornament was more than mere decoration: it expressed a building's soul. Flowing organic forms balanced the linear structure of their buildings while adding beauty and grace. Ornament was integral—*of* the building, not *on* it, as Wright had so famously insisted. Elmslie called ornament the building's "final and logical flowering."

The architect took his cue from Louis Sullivan, who believed that ornament brought a building alive. His mentor's method of creating ornament, known then as conventional-ization, imposed lush nature-based motifs over a geometric grid. Elmslie absorbed Sullivan's pronouncements but admitted: "We had a different way of arranging ornamental forms. I couldn't do as he did. I never copied any of it, strange as it may seem."

"Themes are developed with foils of unending variety," Purcell said of Elmslie's signature style, which dominated the firm's work. His concepts were unique but shared elements not only with Sullivan's work, but also with Art Nouveau, Gothic, and Moorish designs. The underlying theme was always nature—the unifying power of nature—displayed in various combinations of organic and original abstract shapes. Seed pods and leaves were a common element, as were the interplay of square and circle, a distinctive V-shaped motif, and convex and concave abstract forms.

Elmslie brilliantly mastered every variety of ornament: terra cotta, art glass, sawn wood, stencils, and textiles. Each item echoed a house's broad design concept and was designed specifically for that house. As Elmslie stated, "There should be in any conception only one idea, one theme, one purpose." Terra cotta (Latin for burned earth) was a specialty but was seldom used on house designs. The Powers House of 1910 in Minneapolis was an exception. Here sumptuous deep green leaves and berries modeled in clay adorn the doorway, while an elaborate terra-cotta spray of orange, green, and blue arabesques festoons the fireplace, repeating themes found in colorful stencils ringing the rooms.

In other houses, wood sawn into elaborate delicate shapes embellished entryways, screens, fireplaces, and built-in and free-standing furnishings. Patterns were carved into furniture, woven into carpets and curtains, and incorporated into stencils. "How our draughtsmen enjoyed inking in these fresh new forms," Purcell recalled. "How hard they tried, without success, to imitate Mr. Elmslie's beautiful singing line."

None of this would have been possible without the talents of skilled artisans and artists who translated Elmslie's two-dimensional drawings into three-dimensional reality. These included Kristian Schneider of the American Terra Cotta Company, who was trained by Sullivan; the metal craftsman Robert Jarvie; and the glassmaker Edward L. Sharretts. Murals and sculpture, often an integral part of the ornament, were designed and executed by a group of compatible artists, including Charles Livingston Bull, Albert Fleury, John Norton, Richard Bock, and Alfonso Ianelli (the latter two Wright associates as well).

Elmslie's organic decorative schemes are among the most exquisite ever conceived by a Prairie School architect. "I suppose I was a transmitter of some kind to add a little beauty to this old earth," he remarked in his familiar, reticent way. Purcell was much more forthright about his partner's contribution: "What George Elmslie did was really poetry."

Elmslie conjured up designs from his own imagination, merging organic and abstract forms into wholly orig-inal concepts. He worked brilliantly in every medium—wood, terra cotta, metal, glass, and paint among them, as seen in the art glass cabinets and stencils of the Powers House (1910) (opposite). Sawn-wood features might erupt from a planter or dance around a room. The end of a window box at the same house is marked by an elab-orate scrollwork finial (top). A decorative V bids an artistic welcome at the door (above).

ETHEREAL ART GLASS

Glass became a magical material in Elmslie's hands—yet another means of unifying a home's interior design. His art glass designs danced along windows, doors, light fixtures, and cabinets in a sparkling array of colors and patterns that repeated motifs found throughout the house: diamond shapes, the circle and the square, and fluid confections of Elmslie's own imagination. This ethereal glass became his signature in nearly every house the partners designed.

Purcell also tried his hand at stained glass. For the 1909 home he designed for his father, Charles, in River Forest, Illinois, he produced art glass panels for the entrance, the dining room cabinet, and the tympanum in the smoking room. But when Elmslie joined the firm, Purcell willingly bowed to his partner's brilliance.

In spinning out art glass designs, Prairie architects rejected the excesses of the Victorian age. Frank Lloyd Wright's clean linear designs set the standard for restraint, while Elmslie staked out a middle ground. As Louis Sullivan's chief draftsman for nearly two decades, he was deeply influenced by his mentor's swirling, nature-based ornament. He embraced this approach, reinterpreting Sullivan's forms into fluid geometric patterns. Yet even when he chose a more flowing motif, he placed it on a field of simple geometric glass. Often he selected purely linear patterns for an entire house, favoring diamond shapes in many cases.

Each window was a complex design composed of hundreds of pieces of glass held together by thin bars of zinc or lead. Colors chosen for individual glass pieces could be subtle or intense. Again, this was a lesson from Sullivan, who was fascinated by the hues of nature found in flowers, trees, and grasses. Elmslie in turn developed a keen color sense and found a kindred spirit in the glassmaker Edward L. Sharretts, who opened his own company in Minneapolis, the E. L. Sharretts Mosaic Art Shops, after Purcell and Elmslie commissioned several pieces from him. For Elmslie's designs, he reserved the very best art glass with the finest coloring.

In addition to providing glorious ornament for the Prairie-style home, art glass came with other benefits. In cabinets it helped shield contents and harmonize ornamental motifs. In windows and doors it screened interior spaces for privacy, eliminating the need for heavy drapery. More subtle patterns were used to frame views to the outside and were strung together in bands of casement windows. The effect was stunning.

Elmslie, like his Prairie School colleagues, turned to art glass to express a building's inner spirit and integrate a house's design elements. He skillfully reinterpreted this ancient art form for the modern home, proving that, as Purcell suggested, "glass which had been glorified in cathedral windows as a sort of precious jewel could answer also a common need in daily life."

In the Wakefield House (1911) in Minneapolis, Elsmlie placed a V, one of his favorite motifs, onto a flowerlike form set into a field of simple rectilinear shapes (top). Another variant of the V pattern appears at the Hineline House (1910) in Minneapolis (above). The current owners were so fond of Elmslie's motif that they hired a local artisan to re-create the pattern for several windows in the house.

A chosen pattern might appear on windows, cabinets, doors, furnishings, and stencils. In the Purcell-Cutts House (1913), Elmslie turned to another favorite form, the diamond, for art glass windows (opposite). Filled with diamonds, they glitter like gems too. Their subtle colors diffuse light but allow nature to show itself.

Harmonious Furniture

A home could not be truly progressive if its furnishings did not suit the modern lines of the architecture. Purcell and Elmslie quickly discovered this problem when clients moved in their jarring Victorian heirlooms. As Purcell lamented: "The furniture was so inharmonious and out of step with the fresh clean design of the rooms. . . . The day when one could go to the shops and find acceptable furniture of living form, fabric and color to harmonize with clean, honest design, was still thirty years ahead and we continued to be distressed with house after house as the people moved in with their lifelong accumulations."

So Purcell and Elmslie, like Frank Lloyd Wright on the prairie and Greene and Greene in California, custom designed their own furnishings. This gave them more stylistic control over the final product and helped harmonize the overall design. Pieces were often embellished with a unifying motif to make them integral parts of the whole. Sometimes the unifying element came from the architecture itself: for a cube-shaped bank, Elmslie designed a cube-shaped chair. Elmslie's furniture was generally more ornamented with inlays and carved organic forms than the work of other Prairie School architects. Purcell tried his hand at furniture design, but after Elmslie joined the firm the new partner generally took on this responsibility.

Most of the firm's home furnishings were built into the architecture: dining room breakfronts, bookcases, desks, cabinets, and inglenooks. Built-ins conserved space and kept homeowners from bringing their own incompatible possessions. Lighting was also integrated. Round globes on pillars of carved oak were set into fireplace mantels, bookcases, and doorways to illuminate a house with a soft glow. Like other built-ins, they fit seamlessly into the design.

The firm also produced freestanding pieces, including sofas, chairs, and dining room suites. The latter became something of a specialty, with tall-back chairs crafted to gracefully frame one's head and make dining a beautiful experience. As a Louis Sullivan protégé, Elmslie preferred flowing, lyrical shapes rather than the strictly linear forms favored by Wright. His chair backs and table top for the dining room set in the Keith House (1910) in Eau Claire, Wisconsin, blossom with fluid abstract motifs. Elmslie was so pleased with the design that he created a similar set as a gift for his wife, Bonnie. Chairs for the 1915 dining suite for Mrs. William H. Hanna in Chicago featured a delicate triangular back that was, according to him, "inlaid with English holly, strips of copper, and gold leaf baked on iridescent porcelain." The shape recalls the V he used in his ornament.

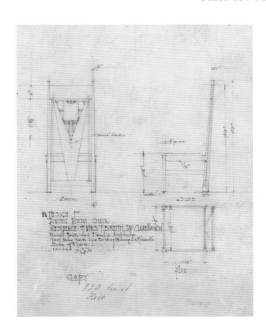

Purcell and Elmslie went to extraordinary lengths to make their furniture not only beautiful but also comfortable. In designing chairs for a Sunday school, they realized that children were not just "small sized adults" and thus were not comfortable in miniaturized adult chairs. As Purcell related, "after considerable measuring of the children and their sitting preferences, measurements were established for four sizes of chairs." Adult homeowners, needless to say, were not individually measured as the children were.

Every item inside the house, from furnishings and fireplaces to the art glass and ornament, contributed to Purcell and Elmslie's plan for a completely unified design. Their goal was to remake the American home to suit the needs of the modern family.

Edna Purcell's writing nook in the Purcell-Cutts House (1913) featured a chair with a distinctive triangular back (opposite). The house's only floral-pattern art glass window was positioned exactly at eye level. For Mrs. T. B. Keith of Eau Claire, Wisconsin, Elmslie in 1910 produced a spectacular dining set with similar chair backs in a sawn-wood V motif (left).

Honest to Goodness

Not long after the turn of the twentieth century, Eau Claire, Wisconsin, was a small town filled with large Victorian mansions built for wealthy lumber barons. It was in communities like this—far from the large population centers of Chicago and Minneapolis—that Purcell and his partners began to leave their mark. Between 1908 and 1915 his firm proposed a new city hall and built a church and community house, a parsonage, and two residences. The showpiece was the home that Purcell designed in 1909 for J.D.R. and Merle Steven.

Set back on a broad lawn to take maximum advantage of views and of course to create a grand impression, the three-story brick and stucco house was built before Elmslie joined the firm. Its ornament comes not from Elmslie's swirling designs but from natural materials and finishes chosen by Purcell. "It's pure Purcell," says the current owner, Paul Lenz, "and demonstrates how the architecture, especially the decorative nature, changed after the partnership formed."

A cruciform floor plan—the firm's first—allowed Purcell to place each major room in its own outstretched wing. Frank Lloyd Wright pioneered this cross-shaped plan with his proposal for "A Home in a Prairie Town," published in 1901 in the *Ladies' Home Journal*. Wright's revolutionary concept effectively broke down the Victorian box based on a foursquare plan and opened up rooms with walls of glass. Purcell amd his partners interpreted Wright's concept and made it their own, first in the Steven House and later in the 1911 Bradley summer bungalow in Woods Hole, Massachusetts, and the now-demolished 1912-13 Decker House in Lake Minnetonka, Minnesota.

Fir, apple, and box elder trees surround the Steven House, which stretches out over four city lots. Under a hipped roof, cream-colored stucco rising above red brick is trimmed in a dark green to accent the angular features of this early Purcell and Feick design. Originally the trim was a reddish brown and the stucco a darker tan color to minimize the contrast with the brick.

Paul Lenz, the current owner, copied the garage design that Purcell used on the Steven cottage next door, enlarging it to hold two cars (above). The brick and grout match the house's own materials.

A Prairie-style sconce lights the entrance, tucked into the corner where the porch and living room wings meet in the cruciform floor plan (opposite).

The Stevens were "very modern, progressive people for the time," recalls their grandniece Jan Marshall Fox, who visited the house often as a child. Not quite a lumber baron, but in the lumber business himself, J.D.R. Steven organized the Steven and Jarvis Lumber Company in 1907 and later operated the Eau Claire Book and Stationery Store, at the time reputedly the largest publisher of books west of Chicago. Merle Steven, a Phi Beta Kappa graduate of the University of Wisconsin and a leading member of the First Congregational Church, was instrumental in securing several local church commissions for the firm. Trips to see "Auntie J. D." were always an adventure, Fox remembers. "The screened porch was really wonderful in the summertime—completely covered and cool. We always had lunch there. It was like magic."

The porch, along with other wings of the house, extends out from the central hearth. Each wing is wrapped in glass or screens on three sides for maximum light and airflow. "When all of the screens are on in the summer, it's just like being outside," Lenz notes.

Throughout the first floor, interior walls seem to vanish as rooms share corners and space weaves in and out. A high slash of mantel over the fireplace extends itself into a horizontal deck leading the eye from living to dining room and, in the opposite direction, from the hallway to the porch. More wood bands wrap walls and ceilings, turning corners, linking built-in cabinets with windows, and emphasizing the horizontal line of the prairie.

"With the fire brought up to eye level, it's like camping outside," notes Paul Lenz of the central feature in the Steven House living room (opposite). Warm oak trim, stained and waxed to bring out its true color, frames the fireplace and continues around the space as a deck.

A partial wall next to the staircase stops short of the ceiling to expand space visually and to provide a perch for a favorite pot (below left). Wood trim adds warmth and distinctiveness throughout the interior (below right). Decorative wooden squares frame ceiling lights.

The dining room stretches out in its own wing, turned eastward to capture the morning sun. A bower of gleaming wood trim and built-in cabinets infuses the room with warmth. Wide roof overhangs permit diners to enjoy their meal with the windows open even when it rains.

A third wing holds a sewing room and the kitchen, which Lenz has given a vintage facelift. Using the original cabinets as a guide, he has added more storage. An antique stove, green and white floor tiles—laid in a rope design to duplicate the trim overhead—and original lighting imbue the room with a comfortable period feel.

In the period-style kitchen (above), modern conveniences are tucked out of sight; the dishwasher is behind a cabinet, and a small television in a 1930s Firestone radio tops the refrigerator. A vintage gas stove in cream and green set the color scheme for the kitchen restoration. The floor and counter tile were laid in a rope pattern to complement the wood design of the living room ceiling.

A ledge continuing past the fireplace mantel, rather than a door, marks the entrance to the Steven House dining room (opposite). Here built-ins include a glass-front buffet (right top), as well as covers and cabinets obscuring radiators beneath the windows (right bottom). As earlier Arts and Crafts designers liked, the oak's natural grain supplies natural patterns. An original four-light chandelier hangs over the table, which was built by Amish woodworkers.

Built-in cabinets offer ample storage in the master bedroom (opposite). New furniture, made by Wittmer Furniture, of cherry stained to match the original amber shellacked birch woodwork fits in unobtrusively. Set into its own wing just above the living room, the space is wrapped in windows on three sides. Two of the other upstairs bedrooms have their own sinks, an innovative feature for the time (above).

Upstairs are four bedrooms: one each for the Stevens' two boys, David and William, plus a large master bedroom and a maid's room. On the house's lowest level, beneath the living room but still above ground, the boys had their own playroom with a fireplace and large windows looking out on the yard. The signatures they once carved into the woodwork are still visible.

In 1909, just before Steven commissioned his own home, he hired the firm to design a house for his mother and sister on the same property. Purcell described this four-bedroom cottage as "a simple development in clapboards" with a "nice plan." He based it on a design that he drew for the *Ladies' Home Journal* the year before. After the property was later divided, in 1955 Mary Tomashek purchased the cottage and the garage that once served the Steven house. She has lived in the house ever since.

About the same time the Steven House was planned, a neighbor, Mrs. T. B. Keith, invited the architects over for a visit to ask if they could modernize her Victorian house. Elmslie, who had then joined the firm, produced a dazzling dining room suite with elaborate sawn-wood seat backs. It was such a success that he made a similar set for clients E. L. Powers and Josephine and Harold Bradley and for his wife, Bonnie. After Lenz purchased the Steven House in 1997, Mrs. Keith's daughter-in-law, Gladys Keith, offered to sell him the dining set. "I'd love to buy it," he told her, "but it belongs in a museum." It is now on display in the Minneapolis Institute of Arts, a gift from the Keith family that represents the only complete surviving example of this stunning design.

RISING STAR

■■ Charles Purcell House, 1909 · River Forest, Illinois

Charles Purcell was instrumental in his son's success as an architect. Not only did he help finance William's architecture practice in Minneapolis, he also commissioned the fledgling firm to design a house for himself in River Forest. To create such a house, say the current owners, William Gray Purcell "must have loved his father very much."

River Forest is a stone's throw from Oak Park, the Chicago suburb where Frank Lloyd Wright built his own home in 1889 and where Purcell grew up. Even as a teenager, he was impressed with Wright's work and walked the neighborhood after school watching as each new and dazzling Wright house took shape. The Winslow House (1893) in River Forest particularly stood out. "I knew and loved this house from my High School days," Purcell later recalled. But after college, when Purcell "to please my father" was apprenticed to the architect E. E. Roberts instead of Wright, the famous architect considered him a "lost soul."

Designing a house for his father in this area so dominated by Wright's work gave Purcell an opportunity to prove himself. The design did not come easily, but he considered it a matter of pride to solve the problem without help from Elmslie, who was still with Louis Sullivan. "Had a difficult time developing this design and had no time to get help from G.G.E. [Elmslie]," Purcell wrote. "Indeed the project had given me so much trouble finding a solution that it became a matter of conscience not to retreat from it and to accomplish the result unaided."

Purcell found the key in a simple house that appeared in the *Ladies' Home Journal,* a design by his friend and former Wright draftsman Charles E. White. Purcell used "nothing of White's plan but the general room relation was retained." It also, he suggested, helped him rein in costs. Whereas White's house was estimated at $4,000, Purcell's came in at about $13,500—apparently an affordable price for his wealthy grain merchant father. The generous budget allowed for further embellishments after Elmslie joined the practice. In 1915 art glass windows and doors, new rugs, curtains, light fixtures, and numerous sawn-wood features were added.

With its deep, slightly flared eaves and low, gabled porches and dormers, the handsome three-story house possesses a Japanese sensibility. The roof projects dramatically over the walls for that sought-after Prairie sense of shelter. Purcell had a fondness for high, pitched roofs, as well as for color. Rather than the strongly contrasting light stucco and dark trim seen today, Purcell specified deep greenish gold stucco over red brick with a slate blue roof. Such bold, rich colors were in keeping with lessons learned from Sullivan. Purcell later tried to re-create the color scheme by painting over a photograph of the house to show how it was meant to be.

Walls of creamy stucco stretch above a sturdy red brick base in the house that Purcell designed for his father (right). Purcell composed the house without assistance from Elmslie. After the older architect joined the firm, he designed art glass windows, sawn-wood decoration, and light fixtures. The garage's gabled roof and brick-and-stucco walls echo the house's design and materials (above). "This was the first of our dwellings with a planned-for garage," Purcell recalled later.

A built-in bench, fret-sawn screen, and handpainted mural draw attention to the fireplace (left). Elmslie designed both the screen, which replaced a simple spindled one, and the corner ceiling light. The mural was painted by Albert Fleury, an artist who also worked with Louis Sullivan. Elmslie devised art glass patterns in elegant, flowing shapes that became his own personal signature (above).

Like Wright, Purcell strove to break out of the rigid Victorian residential box. Here he did this by treating the first floor as one room. Large openings between the living and dining rooms and glassed-in veranda with French doors vanquish closed-off spaces and dissolve solid walls. Even the ceiling seems to float above the rectilinear wood molding wrapping the rooms.

For contrast, Purcell carved out an intimate alcove next to the living room fireplace where the family could gather. As an important symbol of home for all Prairie architects, the hearth was often emphasized by adding an inglenook and special decoration. In this house a fret-sawn screen of oak designed by Elmslie, greenish gold tiles, and a mural by the artist Albert Fleury frame the space in nature's palette. The painting, added in 1910, depicts the view Purcell's father saw from the Catskills cabin where he spent time as a child. Fleury taught at the Art Institute of Chicago and also created murals for Sullivan's Auditorium Building.

Opposite the inglenook is the home's star attraction—perhaps the most charming and inviting space Purcell ever designed. Completely encircled in stained glass, the cathedral-like smoking room was created as a personal retreat for Purcell's father. Elmslie's dazzling art glass windows and doors and Purcell's triangular art glass tympanum in the gable add drama while showcasing their different design styles. Purcell and Elmslie were very particular about their art glass. Instead of using a local manufacturer, they turned to the Sharretts Mosaic Art Shops in Minneapolis, a firm they trusted for its fine glass and attention to detail and color.

Three decades later Purcell seemed pleased with his own work. "Even now, in 1941, as I visualize it, this house is fairly undated." He concluded his reverie by pronouncing it "a good home." An early but accomplished house, it takes its place proudly in Frank Lloyd Wright country.

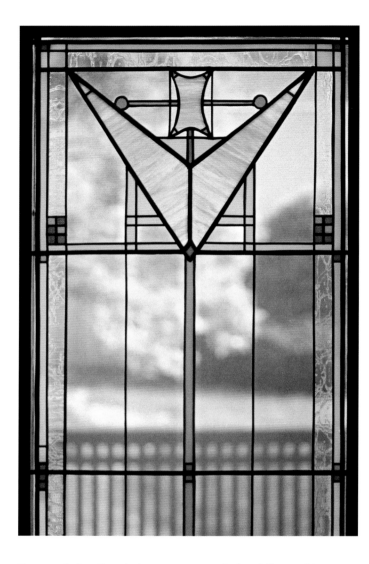

Patterned glass French doors open onto the jewel-like smoking room
(right), which pairs Elmslie's artistry with Purcell's own. Two of
Elmslie's trademark motifs—the splay-cornered rectangle and the V
(above)—are joined in the iridescent green-and-white glass that rings
the room. Purcell's art glass design is set into the gable.

SUBJECT TO CHANGE

When Purcell and Feick opened their practice in Minneapolis in 1907, horse-drawn carriages were the primary mode of transport. But change was in the air. Horses clip-clopping slowly along dusty city streets had to make way for noisy, bone-shaking automobiles. Henry G. Goosman, owner of the leading livery stable in Minneapolis, saw the writing on the wall.

"Old man Goosman, a 'Dutchman' if there ever was one—short, round, bald, jovial and irascible—was wise enough to see the doom of his business and the rise of the automobile," observed Purcell several decades later. In 1907 the liveryman commissioned Purcell and Feick to design a "horseless carriage stable," the first structure in Minneapolis built solely for automobiles (page 24).

It was thus no surprise that the 1,700-square-foot house Purcell and Feick designed for him two years later would feature the first tuck-under garage west of the Mississippi, according to the current owners, Tom Oliphant and Lynn Barnhouse. "It was a fairly radical feature for 1909," says Oliphant. The garage, at the back of the house, is accessed through an alley.

The one-story house itself is something of an anomaly. Perhaps the most fitting description for it is a Prairie-style shotgun bungalow because of its long, narrow shape. It was originally designed to be constructed with a newly patented type of terra-cotta building block. But the cost estimates were so prohibitive, said Purcell, "we went to the expense, for our good friend Goosman, of making a complete new set of revised drawings." The change was drastic: from an elaborate two-story structure of terra-cotta blocks to a one-story wood-frame dwelling with lapped cedar siding.

Beyond a sheltered portico on the right side, a small vestibule unfolds into the living room. "The dropped ceiling in the hall lends an intimacy as one heads into the private areas of the house," Barnhouse notes. To maximize space, the living room sweeps around the central hearth into the dining room. "The open flow between rooms and the spiral traffic pattern around the fireplace were way ahead of their time."

Off the living room a glazed porch stretches the full width of the house, accessed by a pair of French doors that flank a picture window. Wing walls at either end of the porch provide privacy from the neighbors without making the space feel enclosed. "It's such a minimal architectural gesture," Oliphant says, "but it makes such a huge difference in comfort."

Barnhouse and Oliphant are working diligently to rehabilitate the two-bedroom house, which has suffered years of neglect and poor maintenance. "There hasn't been a thing done right on this house since it was constructed," laments Oliphant. Much of the interior trim is gone, as is the inglenook around the fireplace and the original stenciling. The couple, both graduates of the Cranbrook Academy of Art, renovated the kitchen and master bedroom and are restoring the exterior to reflect the architects' original intentions. After finding the diamond-shaped front window—never installed—in the attic, they put it in its rightful place.

Purcell was disappointed that the house could not be built of terra cotta as planned but was pleased with the interior arrangement: "As finally built," he said, "the interior of this house was a very happy group of rooms."

Five windows brighten the front sun porch (top). The entrance is sequestered within a vestibule (center). Yellow and forest green colors used originally have been changed to light gray-green with red-orange accents (above).

Although some original detailing has been lost over the years, the house retains its elegant Elmslie-designed art glass in the dining room breakfront (opposite) and in a cabinet flanking the fireplace.

Not Too Much Architecture

"Ed was a moose of a man in appearance, with handlebar moustaches and an extra serious deportment," Purcell said of the tinsmith Ed Goetzenberger. His first job with the architect was crafting the metalwork on the 1907 house that Purcell designed for himself and his grandmother, Catherine Gray. Purcell and Goetzenberger developed such a close relationship that the craftsman became a regular member of the firm's team.

"He was proud of his business, his home, and his family. . . . When he got ready to build his real home, I was 'the architect who had to do it,'" said Purcell, who prided himself on his kinship with "these common men—the mechanics of the Building Trades." His grandparents had instilled in him this democratic approach to life. "It was a satisfaction to have gained the confidence and respect of these men, for it proved that my understanding of their trade and craft and my feeling for the materials in which they worked was sound. I respected their world, honored their inanimate friends, the wood, the steel, the glass, in which they worked— and they honored me for it," he explained. To Purcell such relationships were "one of the joys of our architecture life."

The men's mutual respect resulted in a straightforward design of great charm, one that Purcell acknowledged "followed logically in the plan trail" of several other relatively low-cost homes of two stories with a high gabled roof and an open plan. The living and dining rooms were placed back to back around the fireplace. "Because these houses of ours . . . are organic and obviously practical in construction and plan, they have a certain Scotch honesty and earnestness," the architect declared.

Lacking the horizontal profile most often associated with the ground-hugging Prairie style, the house seems caught halfway between the progressive movement and vernacular houses of the early 1900s, a fact that Purcell readily admitted: "The house is plain and rather severe, but these types, like the early Colonial houses, provide plain wall surfaces like neutral mounts, against which a gay awning, the flowers and the changing sun and light make atmospheric play of decoration and color, which too much 'architecture' seems to disturb."

Some of the plainness he spoke of may have resulted from the original natural brown stain. "Ed Goetzenberger's granddaughter remembered a dark, dark, dark house," noted Bob Glancy, the home's third owner, after he tracked her down. Friends questioned Glancy's sanity when he bought the house in 1999 as an investment and considered living there. Inside, Glancy recalls, "There were paths winding through piles of debris." The exterior was covered in asphalt siding. "I tore every piece off with my bare hands," he remembers. Underneath, the original cedar siding and shakes were in near-perfect condition.

All the natural woodwork inside had been painted. "I took it all down and ran every piece through a sander four times," says Glancy, a real estate agent and part-time historian. He and his wife, an interior designer, chose the house's refreshing color palette: taupe siding, light sage green shakes, chocolate brown trim, and cream for the windows and details.

The Goetzenberger House, now owned by Joanne Opgenorth and Michael McCarthy, was a project in which Marion Parker played a large role and Purcell gladly shared credit: "Mr. Elmslie had no hand in this house," he said. "Miss Parker and I, alone, hung over the draughting boards and gave it the best we had and it proved on this house a good best."

Beyond the brick fireplace, French doors to the porch invite light inside (opposite). A diamond-shaped window like the Goosman House's (page 64) accentuates the peaked roof (top). A tesseract (four squares of equal size) added later frames new house numbers (center). Art glass near the entrance eliminates any need for curtains (above).

HOUSE OF PLENTY

E. L. Powers, vice president of Butler Brothers (a supplier of variety store merchandise), commissioned Purcell and Feick to design a warehouse for his company in 1907. Three years later he and his wife came back for a home of their own. They were just the kind of clients Prairie architects preferred: well-educated, progressive, and completely open to new ways of building. They provided their architects with a sizable budget and free rein.

The Powers House was the first large residential commission with Elmslie at the design helm. He made the most of the opportunity, lavishing the house with sumptuous ornament. Elmslie's abiding love of nature—its lush colors and shapes—found form in exuberant terra-cotta panels in swirling leaves and berries; in rhythmic organic shapes carved into wood; and in the nature-based hues chosen for stencils and art glass. This tour de force of embellishment secures Elmslie's place in American architecture as one of the great creators of ornament.

The four-bedroom house caught the eye of Allan Amis, an architect, several years ago whenever he would walk by. "I was enamored of the Powers House, with its discreet side entry and strong interplay of vertical and horizontal elements," he relates. Allan and his wife, Ginna, did not waste any time in making an offer when the house came on the market.

The layout had initially stumped the firm. "The site is a special one with its most interesting outlook toward the rear," noted Purcell, underscoring one problem: "the necessity of presenting a satisfactory facade toward the street on the north." Elmslie came up with the perfect solution. He turned the house sideways to fit the narrow lot and then reversed the typical floor plan by placing major living spaces in the back to claim the property's view toward the Lake of the Isles. To Purcell the approach was "revolutionary." As he later explained, "Up to this time, parlors were in front and kitchens in the rear—always done—and that was that." To give the front facade the prominence it needed, Elmslie added a two-story tower with grouped windows and a prominent hipped roof. He admitted that the layout disturbed Purcell, who had to persuade the clients that it was the best solution. "You were a bit averse to showing it because it was too unusual and not likely to suit. However you sold it and all were happy."

The quarter-sawn oak door, incised in a V fretwork motif, leads into a hallway that opens into the living and dining spaces and the stairway (below). Ornament abounds in wood on the porch (right top), in twenty-two terra-cotta tiles with flowing leaves and berries framing the doorway (center), and in cabinetry (bottom). Although its narrow end faces the front, a two-story tower gives prominence to the street side (opposite).

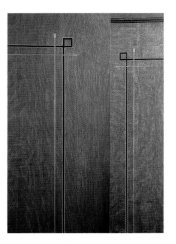

Richly patterned art glass doors (above) open from the sun porch into the living room, with a view of the fireplace beyond. The V pattern picks up the theme begun at the front door. Elmslie turned the motif sideways in the art glass cabinets framing the living room. A stencil frieze pulls the eye toward the incomparable terra-cotta fireplace that fills the inglenook with color (right).

The orientation met with the owners' approval, but they found the design too large and elaborate. At considerable expense to the firm, but no cost to the owners, Purcell and Elmslie reworked the plan and reduced the size. They were stunned at the results. "When the new bids were in, the 30% reduction in size had saved just 4% in cost, a negligible saving," Purcell wrote. The couple nonetheless decided to build the smaller, 3,500-square-foot house, and Purcell and Elmslie learned a valuable lesson: mechanical systems cost nearly the same, no matter the house size. Knowing this allowed them to give clients with smaller budgets more commodious designs, as these would add little to the final cost.

Elmslie's fascination with integrated ornament announces itself right at the doorstep. Here twenty-two bronze-green terra-cotta tiles in a lush botanical pattern frame an elaborate door of quarter-sawn oak pierced with a V motif, one of Elmslie's favorite designs. Such a welcome sets the stage for more embellishment to follow. Beyond the doorway, a low vestibule gives way to a hall that leads to the living room on the right, the dining room on the left, and ahead to stairs up to the second floor. The eye is immediately drawn to the living room, where Elmslie lavished his greatest attention. Recessed beneath a canopy of sturdy oak trim, two built-in benches embrace a generous fireplace crowned in a spectacular terra-cotta frieze framed in green and gold. Organic berries and oak leaves join flowing geometric shapes of Elmslie's own imagination to bring the austere gray brick fireplace to life.

Purcell and Elmslie balanced the tower's curves with an arc of windows and a built-in bench facing the secluded backyard (above right). The opening from the entry to the living room encourages movement into the house's private spaces. Delicately colored stencils once again ring the upper walls. To re-create them, Allan Amis, the current owner, studied Elmslie's original ink-on-linen plans bequeathed by Purcell to the University of Minnesota.

Elmslie's stunning wall of terra cotta on brick calls attention to the fireplace, the home's central feature (opposite and above left). Arts and Crafts designers liked to create cozy inglenooks such as this. A pair of built-in benches and Mission-style rockers keep the focus on the fire and encourage togetherness.

More dazzling ornament is found in the living room's patterned art glass cabinets flanking the generous entrance and in French doors leading to the sun porch. Shimmering stencils in blue, green, orange, and brown ring the room. As if this brilliant display were not enough, Elmslie also provided a curved window seat to take in nature's beauty. The dining room holds its own against all of this, with Elmslie's V-shaped motifs carved into the sideboard and additional stencils outlining the room.

Such elaborate decoration was not always appreciated, Purcell reflected, even by progressive clients who were "at that time so thoroughly drilled by Stickley and his Mission Furniture . . . that it was difficult to secure acceptance of even the most sincere and restrained architectural embellishments." Purcell himself initially thought that Elmslie had gone a bit overboard with the ornament, but ultimately he came to see the Powers House as one of their most successful commissions. "This Powers house," he said, "is a distinguished piece of work, and it still stands fresh and interesting, truly contemporary with the most thoughtful buildings of today."

At the time he wrote those words in the 1940s, even the most minimal decoration was being eliminated from residential designs. Purcell was disheartened, but he predicted a turnaround: "It is inevitable that sensitive designers cannot continue to view Architecture as nothing more than streamlined engineering, but must recognize the spiritual element emanating from utilitarian forms. . . . This will come whenever we reach a point where our enjoyment of beauty is more important to us than speed, everlastingly trying to get to where we don't happen to be." In the Powers House, Elmslie turned simple objects such as doors, cabinets, and windows into timeless works of art that encouraged occupants to pay attention to the dazzling show—an act in perfect harmony with Purcell's admonition to bring forth the spiritual element from utilitarian forms.

Designers such as Purcell and Elmslie felt fortunate when a client commissioned both house and furnishings. Elmslie created an exquisite dining set for the Powers family (pages 30–31), with elaborate carved chair backs and a table, none of which has survived. The house's current owner made a hanging light using remnants of an original lamp found in the basement (opposite). Elmslie's V-pattern art glass appears again in the china cabinet. On the dining room buffet (above left), built-in lights reduce clutter and echo the design of wall sconces.

With its built-in bench and alcove for the piano, the tower's lower level, originally a den, makes a perfect music room (above center). Different stencil frieze patterns signify different rooms. One with an oval motif terminating in a four-part tesseract highlights the living area (above right). The screened porch, keeping the house in touch with the outdoors, is encircled by sawn-wood ornament with a cloverlike quatrefoil motif (below). The four-light hanging lamp, added by a previous owner, picks up the theme.

A Natural

A hair-raising commission for a fireworks warehouse led to Purcell and Elmslie's design of the Hineline residence. "The firecrackers were in transit from someplace," Purcell recalled years later. "The building had to be designed and built before they arrived." Commissioned by Butler Brothers, the corrugated iron-and-timber structure weathered a fierce storm just as it was completed. "The storm scared the wits out of us for fear the building would leak, or fall down, or be struck by lightning," Purcell added.

All went well, and a Butler Brothers associate named Burr became convinced that Purcell and Elmslie should design a house for his daughter, who was about to be married to Harold Hineline. "Burr wanted us to do a nice little house for the young couple," remembered Purcell. (The firm also designed a home for the company vice president, E. L. Powers.)

The Hinelines' two-story home was based on a 1908 Purcell and Feick remodeling of a barn into a house for Arthur Jones, "a very simple project [that] had a great influence on all my later work," Purcell said. "In this little house I made my first detailed examination of the relation of a building to the size of people and the geography of movements."

Almost everything served as a palette for Elmslie's ornament. Side windows shimmer with new art glass in his signature V pattern (above), and crossbeams blossom with abstracted flowers at the entrance (opposite).

The earth-toned stucco over cypress board-and-batten siding showcases the house's simple sculptural form (below). Because no home in this era was complete without a porch, here a single-story veranda branches off the living and dining rooms. A second porch is located in the rear, servicing the kitchen.

Green, gold, and clear iridescent glass outline Elmslie's V in art glass produced by Edward L. Sharretts, the Minneapolis glassmaker (above left). A red brick fireplace with a raised hearth dominates the harmonious and tranquil living room (above right). Walls are painted in a rosy tan hue similar to the color found in the Purcell-Cutts House. In typical Purcell and Elmslie fashion, a sun porch ushers light into this space and the dining room behind it. The swinging door to the right of the fireplace accesses the kitchen.

New art glass in the house's original V pattern makes the stairway glow (opposite), although it cannot match the patina of the old. Windows meeting at corners and the ceiling line visually release space. At the entrance the built-in bookcase serves as a partial wall, screening the stairway from the living room. Small sawn-wood brackets in a quatrefoil design support the fireplace mantel (below).

With the Jones House as a starting point, the architects drew on the open floor plan that became almost standard for their small and medium-sized houses: the living room reaches around a central fireplace, borrowing light and space from the adjacent dining room as well as the glazed sun porch. Although the essentials were the same, each house was tailored to the specific needs of the clients. Here cabinets, doors, and windows are all carefully placed for maximum functionality and comfort—in accord with Purcell's "geography of movements" study. Upstairs, three bedrooms branch off the central hall. Ceiling heights fluctuate from low in the hallway to high in the bedrooms, creating a sense of spaciousness and release.

Despite a modest budget, Elmslie produced exceptional art glass for the house in his signature V motif. The pattern appears on the two swinging doors that lead from the dining and living rooms into the kitchen. Steve Corcoran and Beth Larson, the owners who restored the house in 1995, loved the design and had a local artisan re-create the motif for the light screens that illuminate the stairway up to the second floor. The couple spent several years restoring the 1,900-square-foot house, removing carpet and wallpaper and reinstalling hanging lights and wall sconces. "We found the fixtures stashed in the basement crawlspace," Larson notes.

Outside, as Purcell recollected in the 1940s, the house relates "beautifully . . . to its simple, flat woodsy site." A prominent but low-pitched gabled roof reaches out with exaggerated eaves to bring the dwelling closer to the ground. A row of casement windows at the second story welcomes sunlight into the master bedroom and frames views into the treetops and the sky. The entrance portico, flanked by low brick pillars and topped with a hipped roof, matches the veranda on the east. These pillars, the grouped windows, and the low roof with wide overhangs testify to the influence of bungalows on the Prairie style. Looking back in the 1940s, Purcell reflected that the house "conveyed a deep sense of satisfaction in which self-conscious 'design' seemed absent—in today's expressive slang it would be called a 'natural.'"

STREAMLINED PRAIRIE

Purcell and Elmslie were known to accommodate their clients' needs. Some, however, could not be appeased, and Lyman Wakefield was in a class by himself. His "interest was wholly 'how much house for how little money,'" recalled Purcell. "From the first we were obliged to make a box of it, and then the struggle began."

The architect recounted this story in the 1930s: "One day he got very angry because we couldn't put in all he demanded without his adding dollars to pay for it. He hammered on the draughting board, yelled and swore—scared a room full of draughtsmen right out of their wits. I am ordinarily not very scrappy in such clashes, but this time I came back and told him a few things. Surprisingly he took all I had to say and made no further fuss."

Despite the skirmish, Wakefield received an elegant design in a classic Prairie style, one that still looks surprisingly modern. Its plain stucco exterior, carefully balanced facade and window placement, and broad hipped roof call to mind the somewhat traditional Prairie designs of George Washington Maher in Kenilworth, Illinois, or even Frank Lloyd Wright's more symmetrical Winslow House (1893) in River Forest, Illinois, a favorite of Purcell's when he was a teenager. "Extravagances and caprices of streamline design," he noted of the Wakefield residence, "make even the hat brim eaves seem conventional enough."

A built-in bookcase in Lyman Wakefield's office is topped by a trio of art glass windows that look into the entry hall (opposite). Drawers at the bottom pull out for additional storage. Purcell admitted that Wakefield "was one of the few men I have met whom I thoroughly despised" yet kept his dealings with him strictly professional.

With its low hipped roof, the 4,200-square-foot Wakefield House conveys the sweep of the prairie but with a simpler facade than some of Purcell and Elmslie's other houses (below). Originally the stucco would have been a deep earth tone and the windows and doors trimmed in a darker contrasting shade. Now painted to match the house, Elmslie's sawn-wood decoration still shows its intricate form (above).

The low entrance opens up in the spacious foyer, whose brilliant art glass windows bring interior light into what was Wakefield's office (above). A lone pillar stands in place of a solid wall, providing views from the living room to the office and up the stairs. The lighted alcove at left and the wood trim further dramatize the space.

From a snug entry, space unfolds into an expansive room-size foyer with large openings that encourage easy movement into the living areas of the house. Intricate birch trim divides the space, leading the eye from room to room; its natural wood finish brings the outside indoors with a simulated forest of outstretched branches. Three art glass windows offer a peek into Wakefield's private realm, his office. To the right, four wall-to-wall windows illuminate the landing of the stairway leading upstairs to four bedrooms and a sleeping porch.

The ceiling rises high over the living room, giving it a liberating lift. Double-hung windows are balanced on either side of the fireplace, which is situated—unusually for a Purcell and Elmslie design—on an outer wall. The firm tended to locate the fireplace in the center of a house, allowing an open floor plan by eliminating interior walls. Although the fireplace is in a more traditional position here, the floor plan is notably free flowing.

Like Wright, Purcell and Elmslie knew how to manipulate ceiling heights to change the feeling of a room. Where the ceiling is raised, as in the living room, one feels a sense of release and openness. Where it is lowered, as in the entryway or in Wakefield's office, one feels sheltered and protected. This ability to convey both the freedom of space and the comfort of shelter is one of the Prairie style's key attributes.

Susan Greenawalt, the fourth and current owner, was reared in upstate New York and is more accustomed to colonial and revival-style houses. "There isn't a curve in this house anywhere," she notes. "But I've grown to appreciate the design's simplicity. It's refreshing." Her words nearly echo Purcell's own 1935 retrospective. "It is heartening," he said, "to see how fresh this house looks after twenty-five years."

To link and define spaces, a forest of natural birch beams branches out to frame the house's ceilings, whose heights vary from space to space. The living room (left) shares a wide opening with the entrance hall, making both seem larger. French doors off the hallway lead outdoors.

THE HOUSE BEAUTIFUL

Purcell and Elmslie believed that beautiful homes, furnished with care, could nourish and uplift the spirit. This concept of "the house beautiful" was the cornerstone of the Arts and Crafts movement as well as the goal of Prairie School architects: honest use of natural materials, simplified interiors, grouped windows to fill the house with light and bring nature inside—all contributing to the good life and the good of society.

The residence that Purcell and Elmslie designed for the Owre family clearly met this objective. Built for a doctor, Oscar Owre; his wife, Kathryn Riis Owre; and their children, the house instilled its occupants with a strong sense of place and beauty. Dr. Owre was an accomplished physician; Kathryn was the daughter of the famed social reformer Jacob Riis, whose writings and photographs exposed horrific living conditions in New York City's tenements in the 1870s. Their sons, Jacob and Oscar, both went on to distinguished professional careers.

"You designed something that was perfect for us," Jacob Owre wrote to Purcell in 1955 after his mother had died. "I walked through [the house] and thought what a wonderful house it had been. . . . It is still as fine, as honest and true and rich in context as it was almost half a century ago. I know it has molded my thinking and feeling in many ways, as a beautiful thing must."

Perched on the crest of a hill overlooking the Lake of the Isles, one of a chain of picturesque lakes that run through the city of Minneapolis, the Owres' house is indeed a "beautiful thing." Its clean lines, honest construction, rich wood trim, and stucco walls combine to create a harmonious whole that epitomizes the innovative Prairie style.

Purcell and Elmslie positioned the Owre House on the crown of a hill overlooking a lake to capture the vista (opposite). The glassed-in sun porch was given a prominent position to take in the best views. Casement windows on the second story were grouped for the same reason. A cantilevered ledge above the doorway sports a lovely example of Elmslie's sawn-wood decoration (below left). Rhythmically placed square spindles lend support to the cantilevered soffit above the dining room and living room windows (below right).

The owner's replica of the sofa designed for Wright's Robie House, with its wooden arms and back, and antique Mission-style pieces suit the living room well (opposite and above). Jacob Owre, his brother, Oscar, and their wives spent one last Christmas in the house in 1955 while they packed their mother's belongings. "We had it decorated for Christmas and had the lovely fireplace going, and we left it with a big wreath on the door. The place looked very beautiful, perhaps more beautiful without its furniture and pictures."

The real beauty of this house shows itself inside, where Purcell and Elmslie composed a symphony of simplicity. Wood is treated naturally, stained and waxed to bring out its innate quality. It rings the walls and ceilings to highlight architectural features. It stretches across the house in robust floors, warmed with colorful rugs. Rooms unfold into other rooms with wide openings to encourage freedom and movement. Motifs and patterns are repeated throughout, imparting a unity of vision.

All unnecessary walls were eliminated. Vistas open up within and without. From the glazed veranda at the front, it is possible to look completely through the house beyond the living room, into the dining room, and out the windows in the back. Only the fireplace, with its notched partial wall, interrupts the view, much as in Wright's Robie House (1908) in Chicago. And all around, generous windows bring in light and add a sense of even more space.

Purcell and Elmslie understood humans' competing needs for both freedom and shelter. Even in such open spaces, they turned one focus inward, toward the sturdy brick fireplace. Its simple lines and raised hearth invite everyone to linger near the warming fire. Sofas and chairs are grouped informally. Intimacy with the fire is balanced with views of the lake outside. Overhead, one of Elmslie's mysterious bronze light fixtures illuminates the room in the evening; a second one shines on the dining table a few steps away. Original wall sconces add more light.

An Elmslie hanging lamp reflects indirect light from the ceiling into the dining room (above). Nancy Albrecht commissioned a new dining set with slant-back chairs similar to some of Wright's. Muted wall color in a soft pink blends with the warmth of natural wood and brick for a completely harmonious look.

The kitchen is new but maintains respect for Purcell and Elmslie's original design (opposite). David Heide's new table design is based on period Prairie-style furnishings. The kitchen cabinet design echoes the original cabinetry in the butler's pantry (below).

"I always loved this house," says the current owner, Nancy Albrecht. "It was a little bit hidden and so different from others. You wanted to know more about it." Now she knows it intimately and has filled it with Navajo rugs, her grandmother's Victrola, and her own collection of Mission and Stickley-style furnishings. "I think I bought it because I had all these things the house liked," she laughs.

One of her first tasks was to renovate the kitchen. For this she turned to MacDonald and Mack Architects, the same firm that restored the Purcell-Cutts House (1913) in Minneapolis. Using the original butler's pantry as a model, the designer David Heide re-created the kitchen cabinets to original specifications and restored the wood-panel doors concealing the electrical service and the servant's annunciator (an electric call system indicating in which room help was needed). He also helped with color selection for interior and exterior finishes and paints. The house received several awards for its meticulous restoration, including a 1996 citation from the Preservation Alliance of Minnesota.

Just off the kitchen, Purcell and Elmslie added a maid's room and thoughtfully included a private sun porch for the lady of the house. Four bedrooms are upstairs, three with fine lake views. A large sun porch opens off the master bedroom. "It just cries out for a hanging double bed," Albrecht says. "Even when it rains hard, it doesn't come inside the porch. You can sit out here and get all the breeze."

A few years after the house was completed, Dr. Owre asked Purcell and Elmslie to come back and turn the fourth bedroom at the back of the house into a study. They designed bookcases and a built-in desk with a special drawer on roller bearings that could be pulled out to hold a large dictionary. "It was arranged so that the great book could be left open at the page most recently consulted, and this cut the time necessary to proceed to the next. . . . It was a great success," Purcell recalled in the 1940s. "I always wanted one."

In 1954, the year before she died, Kathryn Riis Owre composed a long letter to "Dear Billy Purcell," describing how much the forty-three-year-old house meant to her. "I . . . truly enjoy just staying in this lovely old house which has become so completely part of my life," she wrote. "I intend to stay here as long as I can, you may be sure. . . . It almost makes me sick to think of ever having to leave it. Perhaps I never will. . . . It has mellowed and softened and is fairly alive with memories of other days and happy times experienced within its walls. A little house I love, so truly a home."

In the landing area adjacent to the living room, steps lead down to the entrance and up to the house's second level (opposite). A built-in bookcase with an art glass front flanks the sun porch; its twin stands on the other side. Wood trim stresses the house's fluid, open spaces. Tall corner windows in the stairwell to the second level break down the walls' solidity and flood the staircase with light (below).

FLIGHT OF FANCY

On a narrow finger of land surrounded by the sea, Elmslie designed the most spectacular house of his career. Built as a summer bungalow for Harold and Josephine Crane Bradley, the house rises dramatically from a water-wrapped peninsula like a great bird ready to take flight. Its outstretched wings—cantilevered floors—hover over side porches. Every room in this 5,000-square-foot Cape Cod house has a sea view.

Clad in cypress shingles weathered to a pearl gray, the bungalow embodies the spirit of both the midwestern Prairie style and the eastern Shingle style. Early in their careers Elmslie and Frank Lloyd Wright were exposed to shingled buildings by their Chicago employer Joseph Lyman Silsbee. A transplant from Buffalo and Syracuse, New York, Silsbee popularized shingle-clad architecture in the Midwest in the 1880s. Wright even designed his 1889 Oak Park home in the Shingle style. Eastern shingled houses shared several features with the Prairie style: an emphasis on natural materials, informal open rooms, a connection to nature through multiple porches, and a rebellion against overwrought Victorian forms. In this commission Elmslie brought the eastern style back to its roots, combining it with the dominant horizontal lines, ribbon casement windows, and open plans of the Prairie style.

The fact that the Bradley bungalow was built at all was "the result of the most astonishing sequence of wishful-thinking" by a powerful cast of characters, Purcell recalled in the 1940s. Josephine Bradley's father, Charles R. Crane, was a wealthy Chicago industrialist with high-placed political connections. He helped underwrite Woodrow Wilson's 1912 presidential bid, served as a special U.S. diplomat to Russia and China, and became deeply involved in Middle East politics. With millions made in the plumbing business, he settled for nothing less than the best for himself and his family.

The Bradley bungalow is clad in southeastern swamp-cypress shingles laid in a horizontal rhythm to echo the landscape (opposite). This Cape Cod house has endured violent storms such as the deadly 1938 hurricane, whose raging seas gobbled up twenty feet of land along the west bank of the Juniper Point Peninsula.

Deep sheltering eaves protect art glass casement windows, grouped in ribbons to take advantage of light and views (below). Prow-shaped porches nestle at ground level for outdoor seating when the weather permits.

As a summer retreat for them, Crane in 1905 rented an 1880s shingled seaside house known as the Butler Mansion in the village of Woods Hole. Five years later he purchased the fifteen-acre estate and hired Purcell and Elmslie to remodel the mansion's dining room and to design stables. The next year Crane summoned Purcell (Elmslie was on his honeymoon) to discuss building a $600 three-room prefabricated cabin on the estate for his daughter and her husband. The discussion took a surprising turn as the limitations of customizing the prefabricated house soon became evident. Purcell later recalled the conversation:

"But we must have a bathroom," Josephine said.

"Can we have a bathroom?" Crane asked.

"Certainly," Purcell replied.

"But Father, there is no porch."

"We can easily add a porch."

"With our two children, we should have a place for the nursemaid."

"Yes, that's true," Mr. Crane said. "And she should have a bath."

Finally Purcell asked why they wanted to build a prefabricated house. Were they in a hurry? No, came the reply. They simply thought that it would be more economical. After more discussion about bedrooms, kitchens, bathrooms, and porches, Purcell persuaded them that they would be far better off with a new house. He returned to Minneapolis and laid out his ideas on the drafting board. "Mr. Elmslie smiled and said, 'Leave it to me. I know just what they want,'" Purcell recalled.

The central curved prow, aglow in the evening light, holds the observatory, as the living room is known. To the left is the west dining porch, which is used for lunch and dinner. The east porch is hidden behind the prow.

Elmslie developed three schemes: a simple one with three bedrooms, two servants' rooms, and two bathrooms; a larger one with each room expanded; and finally a highly sophisticated cruciform scheme with wings projecting from a central hearth holding four bedrooms, two sleeping porches, two main bathrooms, two half-baths, servants' rooms and baths, an enormous living room, a kitchen, two dining porches, and open terraces.

When Purcell showed Crane and his daughter the three plans, the two smaller ones were set aside. "All of the discussion centered about the most elaborate of the three schemes." Almost no changes were made to the plan. Purcell and Elmslie were told to proceed. It was then early April 1911. The Bradleys wanted to take occupancy by October 1, in time for a wedding there. With a nearly unlimited budget, the firm was also hired to landscape the grounds and fill the house with furniture, kitchen equipment, curtains, rugs, and mono-grammed linens.

"On the evening of September 30, the Cranes and Bradleys walked up to a house that looked as if it had always stood on the site, and found within a complete establishment ready to live in to the last detail," Purcell wrote. A few days later, Mrs. Crane's sister was married in the house. "We received a very cordial and appreciative letter, indicating how delighted everyone was with the result," Purcell recalled. They had reason to be pleased. The house was magnificent.

Overall, the summer home measured more than one hundred feet "from tip to tip" in one direction and eighty feet in the other, Purcell recounted, adding, "The total cost of the $600 portable bungalow was $30,000." Throughout, Elmslie masterfully harnessed the beauty of the sea. Full face to the ocean and wrapped in a continuous band of art glass windows, his fifty-two-foot-diameter living room, called the observatory, projects outward like a pilothouse to command spectacular views. Beneath the ribbon windows a curved bench rings the entire outer wall, offering space for at least twenty people to watch the waves crash below. Elmslie balanced nature's performance with masterworks of his own: a massive fireplace crowned by a fan of tapered Roman brick as well as exposed cypress beams that carry exquisite sawn-wood ornament. To protect against hurricane-force winds, he framed it structurally in iron. Vertical bars anchored in cement reach eighteen feet into the earth; cypress-enclosed horizontal beams support the forty-foot-wide observatory and the massive cantilevers.

On the ceiling of the observatory (the living room), exposed cypress beams emerge like the spokes of a wheel from an elegant sawn-wood semicircle (above).

At the heart of the living room, a massive arched fireplace with a tapered Roman brick fan echoes the semi-circular plan of the space (below). Ten pairs of casement windows filled with art glass reach around a great curving prow enclosing the observatory. Elmslie placed tinted art glass only at the windows' edges, leaving the center free to maximize views. A window seat wraps around the outer wall, providing space to watch the ferry on its way to Martha's Vineyard (opposite); radiators are concealed behind cypress registers. Lights built into the clerestory behind art glass panels illuminate the ceiling.

Art glass doors open from the east and west dining rooms into the central hall (above), providing privacy while allowing natural light to flow in. A sideboard and cabinets with built-in light standards are situated behind the fireplace (opposite). Elmslie's lanternlike sconces add more illumination.

The house's cruciform plan allowed Elmslie to take maximum advantage of the site while giving every room a spectacular view. Lateral wings reach out from the central fireplace core to the east and the west—like the arms of a cross—holding bedrooms above and dining porches and open terraces below. The lower east porch, warmed by the morning sun, served as the family's breakfast room. The west porch was reserved for formal dining. Open to the elements, the porches were soon glazed in for comfort, but diners were still surrounded by the sea through large picture windows with views on three sides. On the fourth side, art glass French doors opened from both dining wings into the observatory—making the whole lower floor feel like one immense room.

At one time the dining porches were completely open to nature, but glass was added soon after construction to make the spaces more comfortable. Dinner was served on the west porch (below), with its views toward the sunset and the Elizabeth Islands beyond. The family enjoyed breakfast on the east porch, which also served as the Bradley boys' bedroom.

The kitchen, pantry, and servants' quarters were located in the tail of the cross-shaped plan. Even servants were treated to ocean views, both in the kitchen and in their own private spaces. The upper floor held three bedrooms, the nursery, two sleeping porches, two bathrooms, and one half-bath, all clad in cypress board and batten. The Bradleys' bedroom suite, at the western end of the house, included a large sleeping porch, the nursery, a dressing room, a bedroom, and a private bath. Two other bedrooms were connected by a shared bathroom. A second sleeping porch branched off to the rear. Dave Bradley, one of Josephine and Harold Bradley's seven sons, told Purcell, "It is the best place to live in I know of."

Clad in board-and-batten cypress, the bedrooms feel snug and cozy, yet windows wrap around three sides so that occupants can watch the sea even in bed (above). A copper ceiling lamp forces light upward, enhancing the beauty of the natural wood. New chairs are copies of Elmslie's designs for the Merchants National Bank (1912) in Winona, Minnesota.

More cypress encloses the landing leading to the second story, where two small windows light the way (left top). Elmslie used another of his favorite motifs, a circle in a square, for the light fixture in the remodeled Butler Mansion (second from top). Built-in cabinets sheathed in art glass add beauty and practicality throughout the house (third and fourth from top).

Casement windows fill the Bradleys' summer house with light. The only exception is in the kitchen (opposite), where Elmslie chose double-hung windows to more efficiently draft heat from the room. But even in the servants' areas he did not stint on the art glass or the views. The current owners added new custom-built cabinets to match the originals. The large round Stickley table and chairs are original to the house.

The upper story of the beach house (above left) was remodeled in 1915 as a library for Charles Crane. Grouped windows overlook Little Harbor, where the Bradley and Crane children could enjoy a swim. Elmslie encased the interior in board-and-batten cypress, like the Bradley bungalow, and added a fireplace and four eight-foot-long electroliers.

Built in 1911 before the large summer house, the three-story gardener's cottage (above right and opposite) faces west toward the Woods Hole Passage. In keeping with the original house on the property, it was built in a traditional style with shingled walls and a steep roof. The eaves reach close to the ground, Purcell said, "to give some degree of warmth and friendliness to the building," but they project outward only slightly, "as a concession to the eave-less Cape Cod tradition."

In addition to the seaside bungalow, between 1911 and 1913 Charles Crane also commissioned a gardener's cottage, an ice house, a tool house, a greenhouse, several small cottages, a Japanese bridge, a fence, a pier, and a boathouse and remodeled a floor of the beach house as a library. Only the gardener's cottage (now known as the Tully House), the library, and remnants of the bridge remain. "Prosperity reigns!" Purcell exclaimed as the Crane and Bradley commissions started pouring in. Later would come another major house for the Bradleys—a new home in Madison, Wisconsin (page 163), to replace their 1909 Sullivan and Elmslie–designed Prairie-style house. Purcell and Elmslie also adapted the hybrid Prairie-Shingle form to another elegant residence, the Decker House (1912, demolished) in Lake Minnetonka, Minnesota.

Not everyone was pleased with the seaside bungalow. Neighbors were outraged by its modern features and demanded that Crane tear it down and build a more traditional house. They derisively nicknamed it the "Airplane House" because of its appearance. Fortunately Crane took no notice. Today passengers on every ferry traveling between Woods Hole and Martha's Vineyard can glimpse Elmslie's magnificent melding of the Prairie and Shingle styles. "The Bradley Bungalow on the Point was only startling because its forms were new," Purcell explained. "Basically it grew out of its environment with perfect naturalness and simplicity."

REST A WHILE

Tucked into a spacious lot facing east toward the sun, this compact bungalow exudes domesticity. Charles and Grace Buxton named it Rest A While and had the whimsical message embedded in the home's colorful stenciling. Elmslie was away in Chicago when the commission came in, so it fell to Purcell and their draftswoman, Marion Parker, to design the house. "Together we spent time and study on every smallest arrangement and detail," Purcell later recalled. He declared the result "a perfect piece of articulation . . . functional from every view we could bring to bear upon it."

Charles Buxton, head of a local insurance company and a member of the National Farmers' Bank board of directors, came to progressive home design through the bank's president, Carl K. Bennett. An idealist, Bennett believed passionately in architecture's ability to transform lives and asserted that beauty was good not only for the spirit but for the bottom line. He spoke from experience. The Owatonna bank building he commissioned in 1906 from Louis Sullivan and George Elmslie remains a landmark in early-twentieth-century American design. Bennett's vision for greatness outstripped his pocketbook, however, and he eventually lost everything in a bank scandal.

That such a noble commercial building should be found in a small midwestern town is a testament to clients such as Bennett and architects such as Sullivan and Purcell and Elmslie, who believed that greatness should not be reserved for the privileged. "Many critics said that the Owatonna bank was no bank for a farming community," Purcell observed. "Sullivan said that the farming community of Owatonna was the very sort of community that would know exactly what he was talking about. And they did."

Buxton and his wife certainly understood, living in their bungalow until the 1960s. Purcell found the Buxtons "a very appreciative couple." Like them, Mark Walbran, the home's third owner, also feels fortunate to be living here. He grew up down the street and jumped at the chance to buy the house when the second owners called him about ten years ago. "I bought it over lunch," he recalls. He likes the way the broad roof sweeps over the shingle and board-and-batten exterior, its deep eaves making the small house seem bigger. He also finds the interior plan particularly open and livable.

The first floor holds a large living room, a dining room, a kitchen, one bedroom, and a bath. A sleeping porch, situated like a tree house, offers extensive views of the garden. Although the house appears from the street to be one story, the lot slopes steeply toward the back, permitting two full stories at the rear. This natural feature allowed Purcell and Parker to place two generous private bedrooms on the lower level with full-length garden windows.

Walbran found the house's exterior stencil template and color palette marked on an old shingle in the attic. Using this circle-in-a-square motif, he restored the beltcourse stencil ringing the house above the windows and also brought back the intricate sawn-wood feature near the doorway. Other restoration projects are slated for the house, notably removal of paint from interior cabinets to allow the natural wood to shine through and re-creation of bookcases that once held art glass doors; these were salvaged for display in the windows. Walbran has found the perfect home, he says—a place where he plans to "rest awhile," surrounded in the warmth and comfort implied by the house's charming name.

Vibrant stencils add whimsy and lighten the dark exterior (right top and opposite). Art glass panels suspended in the windows (center and bottom) covered the living room bookcases before they were removed by a previous owner. Mark Walbran plans to rebuild the bookcases but leave the glass hanging in the windows.

Rooms with a View

Since the 1860s Summit Avenue has been the most fashionable address in St. Paul. Two of America's greatest authors, F. Scott Fitzgerald and Sinclair Lewis, called this wide boulevard with towering trees home. Although most of the wealthy families who settled on Summit Avenue in the late 1800s built Italianate, Queen Anne, and other revival-style mansions, by the early 1910s a handful of Prairie houses had cropped up. One of these was the home of Bess J. and Ward Beebe.

Purcell and Elmslie were keenly aware of the importance of the Summit Avenue location and made sure that primary rooms in the Beebe House had good views. "At the time . . . it was one of the most talked about residential streets in America, broad and with beautiful trees; the views up and down the street were valued," wrote Purcell in the 1940s. "So the unusual corner windows looking both ways from the living room were accepted as a fine response towards a choice and expensive location."

Ward Beebe was a veterinary surgeon who, when his practice seemed at a dead end, returned to the University of Minnesota and obtained a medical degree. Bess was the daughter of John Leuthold, a wealthy German immigrant and relative of Louis Heitman, who built a Purcell and Elmslie home in Helena, Montana, in 1916 (page 177). (The Summit Avenue house is also known as the John Leuthold residence.)

The Beebes' house sits regally on a gentle rise. Its large cross-gabled roof with deep eaves makes the narrow structure look broader and visually suppresses its three-story height. Purcell and Elmslie treated the windows like ornaments on the simple stucco walls and accentuated their geometry with bands of dark wood. A large half-circle window nestled into the front peak brings daylight into attic rooms. Casement windows grouped at the second floor welcome the sun. Corner windows offer wide views while eliminating the boxiness of solid walls.

A high cross-gabled roof with deep eaves shelters the three-story Beebe House (opposite). Twin corner windows on the first floor balance the front facade and offer fine views. A half-moon window draws attention upward toward the peak. Wooden brackets incised with an intricate V design help support the corner eaves and offer a decorative counterpoint to the house's rectilinear features (below left). Almost anything could be an opportunity for decoration, including stepped brackets on the front windows (below right).

Purcell and Elmslie's built-in cabinets, dark-toned wood banding, and re-created stencils infuse this dining space with intimacy and homey comfort. The table and a sideboard, not visible, are vintage Greene and Greene pieces, handed down from the current owner's grandparents, who brought them from Pasadena.

A central fireplace is the only barrier between living and dining spaces (opposite). According to Purcell, curtains of "fine cream bolting cloth," matching the stencil motif, once hung at the windows. The rocker and table are vintage Mission pieces. Elegantly patterned glass shields treasured objects in a cabinet (below).

Like the firm's Owre House of 1911 in St. Paul's sister city, Minneapolis, the living room and dining room here flow together around a central hearth with no wall between to block views. Purcell and Elmslie eliminated walls whenever possible in first-floor living spaces to open vistas and increase the sense of space. A glass-enclosed veranda opens off both rooms, allowing them to borrow additional visual space from nature. The second floor holds three bedrooms and a bathroom as well as a tiny library sitting-room with bay windows and a window seat. Purcell described the sitting room as "one of the unique features of the plan" and the house itself as "a charming affair."

David and Martha Anderson have owned the house for more than two decades. "It had been pretty stripped down when we bought it," Martha says. "It didn't have the sense of what a Purcell and Elmslie house should be." Several years ago they renovated "to bring Elmslie in," she relates. Most important, the couple reproduced the original Elmslie-designed stencils that encircle the living and dining spaces and the entrance hall. Situated between stretches of horizontal wood banding, this bouquet of deep, rich colors enlivens the interior spaces and unifies the rooms.

In addition to his colorful stencils, Elmslie created exquisite art glass designs for the bookcases next to the entrance. Glass doors for cabinets and bookcases were used by all the Prairie architects; patterned glass gave them another opportunity to harmonize a home's decorative features with a unifying motif. This house's brilliant ornament and fine craftsmanship make it well suited to take its place on the most elegant street in St. Paul.

Room to Spare

:: Tillotson House, 1912 · Minneapolis, Minnesota

About a block from the Owre House, Purcell and Elmslie designed a similar but more modest residence for E. C. Tillotson and his wife. A restrained budget limited the architects' ability to add much ornament or built-in features, but they produced a well-composed, airy dwelling. It pleased the Tillotsons enough that they lived in the house without making changes for thirty-eight years.

A secluded entrance of dark brown brick sets a somber mood that is immediately put aside once the door swings open. Inside, Purcell and Elmslie eliminated all unnecessary walls to produce a spacious open floor plan. Behind the fireplace, the dining room and kitchen are set back to back for convenience. A sun porch, now wrapped in glass on three sides, invites light into the living room. The house has two other screened porches, now enclosed as well; the back porch serves as a breakfast room off the kitchen, and above it is a former sleeping porch.

"The house has a beautiful circular plan," says Karla Forsyth, who owns the house with her husband, Bill. "People walk in and they love it." Upstairs are four bedrooms and a bathroom; a maid's room and a bath occupy the third floor.

Purcell was gratified that the house turned out so well, especially because the firm was "put to some unsatisfying economies" to stay within budget. The Tillotsons, he added, had only "a very vague and shifting notion" of what they wanted in a house. Purcell was frustrated to learn later that the family had no need for one of the rooms they insisted on including. Eliminating the extra room, he wrote, "would have paid for all the good construction and better equipment which they had been so unhappy to lose."

"We've been trying to bring back some of the historic details," Karla Forsyth notes, adding that previous owners had no interest in the house's architectural value and even removed the fireplace mantel. The Forsyths restored it, remodeled the kitchen back to the Prairie style, took out yards of old carpet, added compatible light fixtures, and commissioned a new dining table based on Elmslie's design for the Goetzenberger House.

One feature they did not duplicate was the sawn-wood ornament Elmslie designed for the front entrance gable. The piece was "made several inches too big for its framed opening," Purcell wrote, so it was omitted. He compensated by hanging the oversized piece in the firm's drafting room and later took it to Portland, setting it into the wall of his own home.

Unlike Frank Lloyd Wright, Purcell and Elmslie often used contrasting building materials on exterior walls. In the Tillotson House (left), they combined dark brown brick with tinted stucco to create ornament just from color and pattern. "The wide windows and positioning of the house on the property use the best sunlight, and we almost feel as if we are living outdoors," says the current owner, Karla Forsyth.

Windows meet at a corner in the dining room (right), dissolving all sense of confinement. "This house has such a welcoming feel: open, airy, spacious yet with intimate spaces," explains Karla Forsyth. The new dining table, based on Elmslie's four-foot-square design for the Goetzenberger House, was enlarged to six feet to seat more diners. The owners designed the Prairie-style light fixture overhead.

FINESSE

Maurice Wolf and his wife were idealists "with progressive and liberal minds, which brought them naturally to us and our work," Purcell recalled in the 1950s. The sophistication of the Prairie style appealed to those who favored new ideas over revivals of historical styles. In choosing the forward-looking Prairie style, the Wolfs—like Purcell and Elmslie's other clients—sought dignity, simplicity, and common sense, not conformity.

The bold Wolf House certainly did not conform to tradition. To eyes accustomed to mainstream revival styles, this house must have been a shock in 1917, the year it was completed. The plan owes much to Frank Lloyd Wright's seminal 1907 design for "A Fire-proof House for $5,000," his update of the classic American foursquare published in the *Ladies' Home Journal*. "To the crude ungainly box Wright had imparted style," explains the scholar H. Allen Brooks in *The Prairie School*. "He flattened the roof, strengthened the cornice, ordered the window openings and married the building to the ground." Wright's plan was so influential among other Prairie School architects that it became almost a vernacular style.

The Wolf house expands on Wright's concept with a geometric simplicity—crisp stucco walls and abstract cubic forms—that look modern even today. Like Wright, Purcell and Elmslie lowered the roof, grouped the windows, and moved the entrance to the side, bestowing the foursquare house with a new sophistication. They opened up interior spaces by eliminating unnecessary walls, imparting a sense of freedom and repose. Originally the house had a low hipped roof, but in 1981 previous owners installed a flat roof when the original was destroyed in a storm. This move conformed even more to Wright's flat-roofed "Fireproof House."

Pale teal trim with creamy tan and gray stucco walls give the house a contemporary appearance (below)—in contrast to Purcell and Elmslie's more traditional Wiethoff House (page 183) just a few blocks away, although both share similar open plans. When previous owners installed a flat roof, say current owners Bruce Albinson and Richelle Huff, they borrowed the vocabulary of Purcell and Feick's Stewart Memorial Church (1909) in Minneapolis. The backyard pool (above), added by the current owners, offers a private retreat. The screened porch, in teal, is also new. The lush flower garden is Huff's handiwork. The couple's son, Walker, enjoys the sunset from the rooftop terrace (opposite).

Inside, the living room pivoted around the central fireplace into the dining room, a concept that Purcell and Elmslie adapted for many other houses. Both rooms opened onto a glazed sun porch. Today, however, the dining room has become the kitchen and the sun porch holds the dining table where the present owners dine almost alfresco. These are among the many changes that Bruce Albinson and his wife, Richelle Huff, have made since they purchased the house in 1993.

In much the way that Purcell in his day sought to create flexible spaces that suited contemporary needs, Albinson and Huff have updated the Wolf House to suit their small family. Professional designers who met at the Cranbrook Academy of Art outside Detroit in 1981, they merged Purcell and Elmslie's concepts with their own modern tastes, transforming the house into a showcase of fine design. "We have taken a few liberties to best reflect our lifestyle," Albinson says, "but have always kept the original Prairie aesthetic in mind."

The living room contains a mix of modern furniture, including a classic black leather and chrome Wassily chair by Breuer, a Saarinen Womb chair and ottoman covered in a dot-pattern fabric by Ray Eames, an oval Saarinen coffee table, and a chocolate brown leather sofa from Ikea (left). Rosy, the family dog, enjoys the backyard view from the new 250-square-foot screened porch (below), which adds to the indoor-outdoor flow of space. Albinson and Huff designed the porch to complement the house's original features.

Designed and fabricated by the present owners, the dining table in the sunroom features a bird's-eye maple veneer with an undulating perimeter over a Saarinen base of brushed aluminum (above left). Overhead is an original hanging light. In the enlarged kitchen (above right), new custom cabinets finished in the same deep reddish brown stain of the originals weave old and new together. Leaded-glass doors from the dining room buffet were also incorporated. Mountain green granite tops counters and the large freestanding island. The two decorative pendant lights were designed by Albinson and Huff, using elements from Elmslie's designs.

An unobtrusive stairway leads up to four bedrooms, a bathroom, and a sunroom on the second floor (opposite, top left and right). Echoing the design of the master bedroom's original glass door, on the left, new sliding closet doors provide twenty-five linear feet of space (opposite, bottom). A similar design was used for the custom head and foot boards. Original Elmslie wall sconces, painted white, illuminate the bed.

The couple eliminated the wall between the tiny galley kitchen and the formal dining room, turning the entire space into a large, modern kitchen. In the living room, they chose crisp white trim and rich brown walls for a clean, casual look and furnished the space in classic midcentury modern, including pieces by Marcel Breuer, Charles and Ray Eames, Harry Bertoia, and Eero Saarinen. Many of the furnishings are production samples collected by Albinson's father, Don, who worked for the Eameses, first at Cranbrook and later at their Venice, California, office. Albinson's parents also met at Cranbrook, attending in 1939 when Eliel Saarinen (Eero's father) was its resident architect and a host of legendary designers were there.

When Purcell looked over the plans again in 1952, he rued the fact that the Wolfs had cut so many corners. The interior, he said, was "unrelieved by any finesse in detail or finish that would have streamlined" its appearance. He suggested that if only the "ultra modern furniture and decorations" then so popular at midcentury could have been available decades earlier, they "would have helped wonderfully to give the room style." Perhaps he was thinking of Eames or Breuer? By blending their own sophisticated style with that of the architects, Albinson and Huff may have added just the finesse that Purcell missed.

Grand Entrance

"I loved the Parker house from the first moment I saw it. I even started stalking it," admits Dr. Peter Thill. "My wife got tired of hearing about it." Her opinion soon changed. "When Karen finally came to see it with a friend, she immediately started to scheme about buying it."

Built for Charles and Grace Parker during the firm's most successful period, the house features one of Elmslie's small miracles: a doorway fit for a king. The architect conjured up a breathtaking entrance of sawn wood that exuberantly welcomes visitors. The house's unclut-tered facade is the perfect foil for this fan-shaped jewel. Sawn-wood features were often part of Elmslie's repertoire but usually played a secondary role. This beauty takes center stage.

Grace Parker seemed to be the driving force behind the commission, and she went to considerable lengths to get her ideas across. "Mrs. Parker has looked over the drawings and the plans seem to interest her very much," Purcell wrote to Elmslie. "The elevation may prove to satisfy her, but she has apparently had the other system of roofing pretty definitely in mind and tells me she has drawn out for herself such an elevation a great many times."

Purcell's letter describes a low hipped roof, but Grace Parker's vision must have influenced the change to a pronounced high gable. Although Frank Lloyd Wright might have balked at such client interference, Purcell and Elmslie welcomed suggestions. As Purcell related in 1949, building owners "were not just clients but partners in the enterprise." Mrs. Parker had other ideas fixed in her mind: "The terrace with steps at the right end and a curving walk passing between . . . two of three cedar trees. . . . The sun room must not project beyond the front line of the house. The wall of the terrace must not exceed one foot in height above the terrace platform, the idea being not to cut off the view of the flower box."

The house is indeed reached by a curved pathway that leads through a grove of towering tamarack (not cedar) trees to the wide, welcoming brick terrace. This low patio does not obstruct the view of the flower boxes, as Grace Parker insisted, and also helps anchor the house to the ground. The sun porch, however, projects about two feet beyond the house's facade, but this placement takes maximum advantage of views.

A high yet broad gable sweeps over the Parker House (opposite), its form neatly echoed on the second gable covering the sun porch and a cross-gabled dormer above. (The attic shed dormer is not original.) The curved walkway was "absolutely fixed" in Grace Parker's mind. Over the doorway (below), seed pods, vines, and swirling abstract motifs explode in a fan of sawn wood, and abstracted coiled ivy nestles into wood squares. One of Elmslie's most poetic designs, it must have been even more stunning in its original multicolored hues.

Past the ornate doorway, a low foyer with an arched ceiling unfolds into the house's major space, the living room. This arched opening offers a refreshing counterpoint to the house's strongly horizontal geometry. Wood banding rings the living room to tie together doorways, windows, built-in benches, and the fireplace to reflect the prairie's simple lines. The ruddy brick fireplace is balanced on the opposite wall by a row of casement windows that bring a dance of daylight into the airy space. Corner light fixtures in the ceiling are part of the unified whole.

Unifying the design inside and out, the same brick is used on the house's exterior and on the massive brick fireplace (left). Pairs of square wood pillars support the simple mantel, and original ceiling lights mark each corner of the room. The child's rocker is an antique Stickley; most of the other furnishings are vintage Mission style. Next to a screen of square oak spindles is a wood box handcrafted by Karen Thill's father (above).

Floor-to-ceiling slatted wood screens help define the arched entry. A small desk tucked behind one screen provides space to work next to a large window offering air and light. Sconces throughout are simple bulbs.

Featuring splayed-corner rectangles, an Elmslie trademark, art glass French doors open from the sun porch into the living room. The original plans specified art glass for nearly all windows, but in the final design it appeared only in the front door, porch doors, and bookcase doors (a fireplace mosaic was also eliminated).

Across the living room the eye is drawn to a pair of extraordinary art glass doors that open onto a spacious, sunny veranda wrapped in large windows. It might look nearly impossible to raise such heavy windows, but these are a cinch. Mounted on tracks, they open by being pushed down into the basement, aided by heavy counterweights hidden below. This engineering marvel, apparently used only on the Parker House, still functions perfectly.

The transition between the living and dining rooms is marked by a generous opening (left). Two bands of trim ring the dining room walls, one tracing a path along the ceiling; the other connects the tops of windows and door frames. Screens of square wood spindles conceal a pair of radiators and form an alcove enlivened by a band of three square and two small rectangular windows.

A wide opening—offering the unobstructed flow of space preferred by Purcell and Elmslie—introduces the dining room, just off the living room. The kitchen is tucked into the remaining corner of the lower level. On the second floor three bedrooms radiate off a central hallway with a tented ceiling, a favored Purcell and Elmslie treatment for upper floors. Seven casement windows banded together at the front of the house bring maximum visual impact and light into the upper floors; five of these open onto the master bedroom to allow views into the treetops, while the other two serve a smaller room. Two more bedrooms are tucked under the gable on the third floor.

Purcell always worked to make sure that his houses were attuned to human needs and comfort. Here he took great pains with the stairs, engineering them for maximum ease. "We were always very careful with stairs," he wrote on the back of a photograph of the Parkers' home. This also pleased Grace Parker. On the same photograph he added, "Mrs. Parker said, 'I will identify any Purcell and Elmslie house blindfolded if you will let me walk up the stairs.'"

Two art glass bookcases in a tulip pattern flank the French doors leading to the porch (below). The colored glass has acquired a lovely patina over the years. Sadly, the front door's glass panel was removed at some time.

HOUSE CALL

Winona, Minnesota, is another of the small midwestern towns where the Prairie style left a mark. In the early 1900s rival bankers, eager to demonstrate their progressive ideals, commissioned several Prairie-style buildings for this bustling community along the Mississippi River. George Washington Maher, who worked in Joseph Lyman Silsbee's office with Wright and Elmslie, designed three buildings here, including the Winona Savings Bank (1914). Purcell and Feick's sketches for a new First National Bank were rejected in 1907, however. But in 1912, with Elmslie on board, First National's rival, the Merchants National Bank, commissioned a new building from the firm. Hailed for its brilliant design and integrated ornament, this bank (page 28) remains a beloved Winona landmark.

Purcell and Elmslie believed that bank buildings should not be rigid, formal, and lifeless but rather beautiful, functional, and inspiring. They brought those same ideals to their design of Dr. J.W.S. Gallagher's house on a broad city lot not far from the historic downtown. Unlike other designs of theirs, here the living room and dining room do not pivot around the central fireplace; instead they sit back to back, as in the Adair House (page 156) in Owatonna, Minnesota, and Charles Purcell's home (page 58) in River Forest, Illinois, both Purcell's conceptions. French doors screened with sparkling art glass showing off Elmslie's trademark V motif open between these spaces and onto the side porch off the dining room. Flanking the raised brick fireplace in the living room are square pillars that were once topped with globe fixtures like the ones in the entrance hall. Three bedrooms, a sleeping porch, and a bathroom are upstairs, and a maid's room occupies the third floor.

To welcome visitors Elmslie left his decorative mark in an ornate carved tympanum in the entrance gable. Beneath the side-gabled roof, walls of tinted stucco rise three stories. An unusual octagonal bay pushes out from one corner, adding spaciousness inside and distinction to the house's profile outside. "I think it is rather interesting the way my own basic ideas about bay windows worked out into this octagonal bay on the corner . . . ," Purcell reflected on his work. "It was an interesting variation on the ordinary corner window idea."

An unusual corner bay balances the triangular gable over the entrance (below). Wood trim calls attention to windows grouped to maximize light (above). Sawn-wood detailing in swirling organic shapes highlights the entrance gable (opposite), which is supported by square brackets embedded with more Elmslian ornament.

Partial screens of square spindles guard the entrance and provide perches for integrated lighting (above). High grouped windows in the hallway and the living room to the right add natural light but maintain privacy.

French doors inset with plain and art glass open from what Purcell and Elmslie called the "living porch" into the dining room (right). The firm often positioned a porch off the dining space to draw fresh air and natural light inside. A second pair of French doors separates the living and dining rooms.

The living room and the dining room, behind the fireplace wall, are not joined together in an open plan. Instead the living room flows into an octagonal bay to add spaciousness (below left). Globe lamps once topped the pillars bordering the fireplace. Current owners Allan and Terri Lieder added their own version to replicate the originals, long gone. A Stickley bookcase and a vintage child's rocker fit in well. High windows light the staircase (below right). Adding a sense of greater space, a spindled screen does not quite reach the ceiling.

Down to Earth

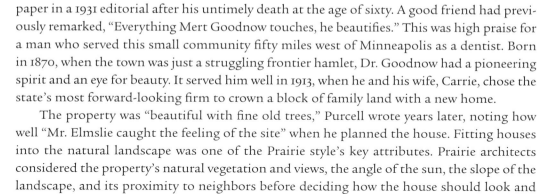

"Merton Goodnow had the soul of an artist," noted the Hutchinson, Minnesota, newspaper in a 1931 editorial after his untimely death at the age of sixty. A good friend had previously remarked, "Everything Mert Goodnow touches, he beautifies." This was high praise for a man who served this small community fifty miles west of Minneapolis as a dentist. Born in 1870, when the town was just a struggling frontier hamlet, Dr. Goodnow had a pioneering spirit and an eye for beauty. It served him well in 1913, when he and his wife, Carrie, chose the state's most forward-looking firm to crown a block of family land with a new home.

The property was "beautiful with fine old trees," Purcell wrote years later, noting how well "Mr. Elmslie caught the feeling of the site" when he planned the house. Fitting houses into the natural landscape was one of the Prairie style's key attributes. Prairie architects considered the property's natural vegetation and views, the angle of the sun, the slope of the landscape, and its proximity to neighbors before deciding how the house should look and where it should be placed.

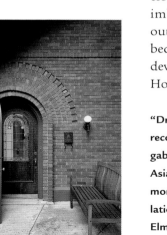

"We wanted to keep the lines of the building as low as possible, because the area of the plan was small and the house was a considerable height above the street," Purcell recalled. Their solution was to stretch the eaves out beyond the wall line to bring the house into a closer relationship with the ground. The exaggerated eaves stress the sense of shelter and imbue it with a calming Japanese sensibility. Purcell and Elmslie liked the way the outstretched roof seemed to suppress the house's height, but it posed a problem inside because the second-floor windows had to be low. Purcell and his colleague Marion Parker developed a standard window height of five feet, eight and one-half inches for the Goodnow House, and this was used on every house thereafter.

"Dr. Goodnow, a dentist, was a man of ideals who was eager for a work of worthy architecture," Purcell recounted. Red brick walls anchor the house and give it a muscular permanence (opposite). Elmslie's shallow gabled roof reaches low to the ground; its deep eaves reinforce the sense of shelter, while brackets lend an Asian sensibility (left top). A fan of brick embraces the arched entryway (left center) and calls attention to the monogrammed _G_ for Goodnow on the door's art glass (left bottom), one of only a few such art glass installations in the house. The garage was built in 1921 (below). "We have no record [that] it was a Purcell and Elmslie design," says owner Jim Fahey, "but whoever did it did a perfect job in matching the home, right down to the interior plaster." Rhythmically spaced northern white cedars contribute to the pleasing composition.

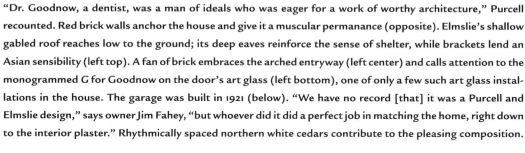

The main living quarters are elevated up a short flight of stairs. Pocket doors open here to reveal a large, light-filled living room with a sturdy brick fireplace—the same brick used on the outside to maintain the unity of design. The room stretches out to the veranda at the front of the house through a wall of glass doors, a technique that Purcell and Elmslie employed often to break out of boxlike rooms and add to the sense of spaciousness. The art glass was missing from the cabinets flanking the fireplace when Jim and Linda Fahey, the home's seventh owners, bought it in 1998. A previous owner helped them find the missing pieces, which are now back in their rightful place.

Bifold doors with clear glass open from the sun porch into the living room (below left), adding light and a feeling of greater space to each. All elements in the house were designed as part of the whole. For greater harmony, the same brick is used on the fireplace and the exterior of the house. Natural wood trim emphasizes the horizontal line of the prairie. The new Stickley sofa offers a welcoming spot to enjoy the fire.

Built-in art glass cabinets flank the fireplace, balancing the design (below). Embedded oak pillars were intended to hold lights with globe shades. Perhaps Merton Goodnow did not like that idea; the lamps were never installed, say the current owners, who replaced the missing glass in the cabinets.

To replace missing doors, the Faheys added patterned glass doors from a house of the same era in St. Paul. One leads into the dining room (above left). There wood banding integrates the built-in breakfront with the windows and a mirror (above right). The windows' large size yields plenty of daylight. A Nebraska house supplied the hanging lamp. The new dining set was handcrafted by Amish furniture makers in Ohio.

The living porch, as Purcell called it, received a tented ceiling to visually expand the space (opposite). Clear glass rises up to the peak and surrounds the room, annexing sunlight and views of nature. Bifold doors with large panes of clear glass divide the porch and the living room but can be pushed back completely so that the rooms merge into one space. Even when closed, the clear glass makes the porch part of the living room.

In the adjacent dining room, a built-in breakfront and a complex system of wood banding give the room a sense of graciousness and warmth. These attributes were not immediately evident when the Faheys started tackling the restoration. "The inside of the house was covered in Victorian wallpaper when we bought it," Jim recounts. "We scraped and scraped and scraped. Fortunately, we have four children to help. Some are still speaking to us," he laughs. Underneath, the plaster was in near-perfect condition and also revealed something else: "We could see the original woodwork placement drawn on the wall," Jim says.

Carrie Goodnow's sewing room is tucked off to the side of the dining room. The kitchen, now updated with new cabinets and flooring, is set into the house's back corner. A narrow staircase for the maid leads upstairs, where she had her own room and sink, and down to the basement, where she did much of her work. Purcell and Elmslie designed a far more generous stairway for the Goodnows, with a landing as large as a room and a built-in oak light standard to illuminate the way. Three small bedrooms and one large one occupy the second floor, which also holds a sleeping porch at the rear. The bathroom, luxurious in its day, originally featured a nine-head shower; a heated tank in the attic ensured a steady supply of hot water.

The house has undergone many changes throughout the years yet still retains the *G* for Goodnow in the art glass entrance door. "From the outside the *G* is backwards," Jim points out, but it reads correctly from inside. Now beautifully restored, this residence remains the pride of Hutchinson, as Merton Goodnow had planned.

Roomy stair landings offer space for a slatted wood settle and a desk (above and below left). A globe-topped pillar lights the way upward. The current owners added the glass door and stencils lining the stairway.

New fixtures update the bathroom but retain a vintage appearance (below right). A warm reddish sienna was chosen for the walls. Stripped of wallpaper, bedrooms are now painted in natural hues (opposite). The ceiling light fixture came from a 1913 Craftsman-style house in North Mankato, Minnesota.

The Little Joker

If any house perfectly embodies Purcell and Elmslie's thinking on the modern American home, it is the residence they composed for Purcell's own family in Minneapolis. "It was a brilliantly successful project in every way and stands today [as] perhaps the most complete dwelling we ever did together," Purcell said in 1915 of his collaboration with Elmslie. Tailored to perfectly suit Purcell, his wife, Edna, and their two young sons, James and Douglas, it has all the classic features of the Prairie style. A low, flat roof with wide overhangs, grouped art glass windows, and dark cypress trim stress the quiet horizontal line of the prairie. Integrated furnishings and ornament, a soft color palette, pale oak trim, and a spacious, open floor plan create a harmonious visual flow within the house.

With financial help from his father, Purcell purchased a prime lot just northeast of his grandmother's home (Catherine Gray House, 1907), near one of the city's picturesque lakes. The property was long and narrow with a lake view to the west. To maintain privacy, Purcell set the house well back of his neighbors so that he would see into their gardens rather than their windows. Then he put his own garden out front. A reflecting pool with water lilies and a small gurgling fountain, designed by the landscape architect Harry Franklin Baker, brought the sounds and sights of nature close. Shade trees, vines, and flowers filled out this urban Prairie garden.

Purcell had a lifelong fondness for high pitched roofs, but when he designed his own home with Elmslie he chose a flat one. Hovering over dazzling walls of glass filling the second story and the ground level, the roof seems to float on air (opposite). A prairie water garden, not visible, unites the house with nature. On the elaborate sawn-wood beam ends near the entry (below left), Elmslie added a humorous reference to Purcell's grandparents: "Gray Days and Gold." The sheltered entrance establishes a transition between the public world and the private universe inside (below right); second-story windows with diamond-patterned glass hover above. Between 1987 and 1990 Purcell's home was restored and furnished by the Minneapolis Institute of Arts, led by the restoration architects Stuart MacDonald and Robert Mack.

Light oak trim and furnishings create a calming effect inside (right). Coordinated colors, materials, and motifs seem to visually expand spaces. A prow-shaped cabinet marks the subtle transition between floor levels.

Inside the two-story, 3,200-square-foot stucco-and-wood house, Purcell and Elmslie broke down the Victorian box in a refreshing new way. Space is molded not by walls or even screens but by changes in floor level. The dining room floats eight steps over the living room, which rests just below garden level. One vaulted ceiling stretches over both. The raised dining room thus becomes a secluded sanctuary, while the lower living room bursts with light and a sense of freedom. "In this dwelling the useless division between . . . sun room and living room quietly slipped away," Purcell explained in 1915. "A new place appeared within the house, all free and open, filled with soft light, tributary in all parts to the hearth."

Elmslie christened the house "The Little Joker" for its highly personalized, light-hearted ornament, which he designed. Initials *ESP* (for Edna S. Purcell) carved into a wooden post near the doorway playfully fool the eye. Look again, and it reads *P&E* for Purcell and Elmslie. Another sawn-wood feature bears the motto "Gray Days and Gold," a reference to Purcell's grandparents, the Grays, and humorously to his father's financial support ($14,000—enough, said Purcell, "to do it right"). Most charming of all, twin sidelights flank the front door with art glass forming the words "Peek A Boo," one to be viewed from inside, the other from outside.

For the rest of the art glass, seventy panels in all, Elmslie chose a diamond shape to enrich windows in the living room, dining room, and upper floor. Maintaining design unity throughout, diamonds also embellish cabinets and appear in tent-shaped shades over standing lamps and in some furnishings. Stencils, some repeating the diamond motif, ring the house inside and out, adding colorful counterpoints to the buff-toned stucco outside and what Purcell called the "rose chamois" walls inside.

A pair of sidelights at the front door of "The Little Joker" show that the architects enjoyed their work (below left). "Peek A Boo," they tease—vanquishing any notion of Victorian stuffiness. One of Elmslie's many diamond-patterned windows diffuses the light in a corner of the house (below right).

At the heart of the living room is the fireplace, a masterpiece of design. Sweeps of arched and linear bands of wood, designed by Elmslie, replace the customary mantel above the hearth. The artist Charles Livingston Bull filled the spaces in between with a stunning mural of Louisiana blue herons rising with the moon in shades of ochre, blue, and purple. With chairs gathered close to the fire and iridescent glass shimmering in the mortar joints, the fireplace's raised hearth offered the perfect perch for breakfast treats, as Purcell recorded in "Own House Notes," his musings on family life written around 1915: "On fine Minnesota winter mornings when the first level sun rays come slanting over the snowy house tops just at breakfast, the table time and again is laid in front of the living room fire. The electric toaster sits on the end of the hearth and the coffee and cheese and jam come down from the kitchen above at their leisure." The hearth also served double duty on Sunday evenings, when the family gathered with "milk and cookies and apples" to share stories "with the firelight for company."

The living room showcases the firm's expertise in tailoring design to specific circumstances. Fourteen-foot-tall windows wrap around the eastern end of the room, vanquishing corners and permitting expansive garden views. Deep eaves on the roof project seven feet outward to protect the interior from harsh summer sun while allowing the warming rays of winter's low sun to illuminate the room until noon. In the evenings these tall windows created a different sort of magic. "I have seen the orange red squares of setting sun sending ribbons of light down the whole length of the fifty odd feet of Living Room," Purcell wrote.

After sunset, the living room was illuminated by five pendant lamps with "inverted semi-domes of pinky lavender moonlight," which produced an extremely soft light. When guests came and the entire room was put to use, he and Edna placed "several dozen candles" around. The house was not overcrowded with furniture: A built-in banquette stretched across the living room's east wall. Dainty folding chairs in blue, red, green, yellow, and violet were brought out when more seating was required. A piano, standing lamps, built-in cabinets and a desk, cube-shaped chairs, and a fern stand filled out the large room.

In this remarkable open plan, first-floor rooms are divided not by solid walls but by floor height. The raised dining room in the foreground looks down into the lower living room (left). The prow-shaped cabinet subtly marks the transition (below). Five metal pendant lights with glass domed shades produce what Purcell called a "pinky lavender moonlight"; a pair illuminates the tall dictionary stand. Stencils wrap nearly every wall.

The house is set some thirty feet behind the general property line so that views from the dining room windows would be free of adjoining houses. The vaulted ceiling reaches beyond the dining room to the west, sheltering a large open porch with a lake view. There was no useless space in Purcell's home.

The family took formal meals in the dining room a few steps away, except in the summer. Then the dining table spent "practically all its working hours out on the porch," Purcell explained. The idea of shaking old habits and eating on the porch or in the living room made life more interesting, he thought. "Ten thousand times ten thousand American families dine in the same spot, facing food in the center of the room with their backs to the windows while all the poetry and splendor there is flows by," he remarked. One of the joys of a progressive home was its multipurpose spaces that allowed occupants to enjoy "the playfulness of life."

The dining suite (above left), with its triangular-back chairs, is a copy of a set designed for Mrs. William H. Hanna and made by the John S. Bradstreet Company of Minneapolis. The backs are inset with art glass (above right). A Richard Bock sculpture, *Nils on His Goose,* looks as if it might take flight from the bookcase prow; the piece was based on the 1907 Swedish children's book *The Wonderful Adventures of Nils* by Selma Lagerlöf.

French doors open from the dining room onto an open porch (below left), where the Purcell family often dined. "When what we eat and how we eat it become so important that we can't move the ceremony of it near the window or outdoors, something in life has become unreasonable," Purcell wrote. Next to the dining room, the kitchen (below right) was entered through a spring-loaded pocket door, which the maid activated with her foot.

The second floor holds a guest room, a maid's room, a bathroom, and a large master bedroom suite, designed to be divided into two rooms with folding screens. At the western end of the room, the Purcells slept in twin brass beds, which could be wheeled out onto the sleeping porch whenever weather permitted; a special threshold flush with the floor made the task easier. The eastern half of the room held a child's bed and a low fireplace with a seating area. The built-in bed, added by Purcell in 1915, was a special design for his "little lad." It resembles a sleeping car on a train, with two tiny windows next to the pillow so his son could look outside. Underneath are huge drawers for toys; the footboard holds a bookcase with a folding desk tucked inside.

In the corner next to the fireplace, Purcell contemplated the perfect winter evening with his boys: "Please imagine, next winter each cold snowy night, two little rosy cheeked lads sit candle-on-table eating their prunes and crackers with milk and waiting for father to come home[,] listening to Robin Hood." The entire house was designed to make wonderful moments like this convenient. "One does the beautiful things in this house in a beautiful way because it is easy to do them," explained Purcell.

He and his family called this perfect house home for just three years. In 1917, as the firm's commissions flagged, Purcell moved his family to Philadelphia to take a job with an industrial leather belting company and later put the house on the market. In 1919 it was purchased by Anson B. Cutts and his wife, also named Edna, who lived here happily for many years and did little to alter Purcell and Elmslie's design. Their son Anson Cutts Jr. donated it to the Minneapolis Institute of Arts in 1985. Fully restored and open to the public, it is now known as the Purcell-Cutts House. "The Little Joker" remains the firm's most lyrical effort to remake the American home.

Globe lights float over the stairway like balloons (below left); the open landing adds to a sense of freedom. Art glass windows and stencils bring key design themes even into the bathroom (below right). The only exception to the house's diamond art glass can be found in a flower-motif window near Edna Purcell's built-in desk (page 44).

Upstairs Purcell divided the large master bedroom into two spaces, with screenlike doors covered in grasscloth (above); at left is the built-in bed for one of his sons. The "little boys' corner with its little fireplace" (below right) was a special place for the architect and his sons to enjoy evenings by the fire. The guest room, where the second son is thought to have slept, is furnished with a slatted wooden bed (below left).

THAT CHINESE HOUSE

▪▪ Hoyt House, 1913 · Red Wing, Minnesota

Purcell and Elmslie carefully crafted each of their Prairie houses to suit the homeowners' lifestyles. But as the houses pass into new hands, they remain as comfortable and functional as they were decades earlier. Jean Chesley and her late husband, Frank, bought this house in 1976 from Florence and E. S. Hoyt's daughter Hazel. It suited the Hoyt family in 1913 as it suited the Chesley family decades later.

Situated along the Mississippi River, tiny Red Wing—famous for leather shoes and pottery—is home to dozens of stunning historic buildings. Yet the Hoyt House, with its sleek horizontal lines, broad eaves, and low hipped roof, holds its own amid the Greek Revival, Second Empire, Italianate, and Gothic Revival mansions that surround it. Louis Sullivan's and Frank Lloyd Wright's rejection of such foreign styles found voice in this small midwestern town when Purcell and Elmslie arrived.

"The design ... would be considered ultra-modern today in any community, but in 1913 it was very much novel for Red Wing," recalled Purcell in the 1940s. "The Hoyts rather enjoyed the new excitement of being pioneers in art, and were delighted with the practical arrangement and convenience of their home." E. S. Hoyt was a business leader, having risen from a furniture salesman at age seventeen to president of the Red Wing Stoneware Company. He led the company, nationally known for its sturdy yet beautiful pottery, when it turned to making art pottery in the 1920s, a shrewd move that continues to benefit the company (still in operation today).

The Hoyts' ten-room, 4,000-square-foot house was one of the firm's most lavish. Nearly one hundred diamond-paned art glass windows and Elmslie's intricate sawn-wood designs add historical texture and richness to the modern design. Purcell modestly pronounced the house "a successful dwelling in every way."

A shimmering band of art glass casement windows hugs the eaves like a decorative frieze (left). The reddish stucco—the original color—led neighbors to call it "that Chinese house" after the Hoyts built it. Accentuating the horizontal lines established by the low roof and the windows, the second story cantilevers over a brick base (below). The topmost deep crimson stucco walls blend into the lower story's red brick, its mortar joints pigmented red. Patterned windows on two levels offer panoramic views of the Mississippi River.

Diamond shapes, Elmslie's dominant decorative motif here, sparkle in art glass windows and doors throughout the Hoyt House and throw richly patterned light across spaces including the foyer (opposite). Randomly arranged pieces of yellow, red, orange, and green glass in the borders add a touch of color.

Built on a modified T plan, the two-story house is gracious and open while providing ample privacy. "The house is designed so that one does not feel confined to the room one is in at the moment," Chesley explains. "There is always a view into another room, always a feeling of communication with the adjacent space."

The entrance, sequestered to the side, opens onto a hallway that leads on the left to an intimate library and on the right into the living room. The house's major spaces—living room, dining room, and enclosed porch—are stretched across the front, encircled in art glass windows. "The sun shines in them almost all day long," Chesley relates, "yet their size and arrangement give a feeling of privacy." More of Elmslie's lavish detailing is found in the built-in light standards near the front windows and an original glass mosaic over the fireplace. The kitchen, the only room in the house to undergo major updating, is located behind the dining room, accessed by a doorway flanked by built-in cabinets.

Upstairs, a narrow hallway with tented ceilings opens onto four bedrooms and two bathrooms. Many of the rooms have corner windows, a favorite technique for expanding the sense of space. The maid's room over the kitchen had its own staircase. Ventilators in the chimney and at the rear of the house were an early attempt by Purcell and Elmslie to circulate cool air around the second story.

Brackets appear to support the second-story cantilever but in fact are mere receptacles for Elmslie's decoration (right). An elaborate fret-sawn screen introduces the house's major decorative theme—the diamond (below). Situated in the covered breezeway, the screen gracefully links the house with the garage.

Like a screen, the fireplace divides the living and dining spaces, inviting glimpses into the next room (left). In the glass mosaic mural, a moon glimmers above the burning fire. "The whole color scheme was very carefully related to the Oriental brick which we had bought from Brazil, Indiana, for both exterior and interior," Purcell wrote later. An interior window between the living room and the entrance hall transmits daylight into the deeper recesses of the house (above). Original lamps help illuminate the already-bright living room (below).

A child's bedroom on the second story displays the same diamond-patterned art glass found throughout the Hoyt House (above). A ribbon of windows turns the corner, essentially breaking down the idea of solid walls.

Like the living room, the dining room is a serene and comforting space (opposite). Diamonds sparkle on the built-in cabinets that flank the doorway to the kitchen at left. A simple geometric oak border outlines the junction of wall and ceiling, while more wood screens the radiator behind the dining table.

In 1925, four years after the dissolution of the Purcell and Elmslie firm, Purcell was in Minneapolis when Florence Hoyt walked into his office. "I was just in the building and had to come in and tell you what joy our home has given us these dozen years we've lived in it." This must have pleased Purcell, especially as he was responsible for the design—a fact that he had forgotten until going through some papers years later. "I had always assumed that this Hoyt House, very different from all our others, was essentially Mr. Elmslie's basic concept and design development. It seemed to carry so much of his established feeling," he recalled. A simple sketch in his own hand revealed "the building . . . as it was finally built and with a surprising amount of specific detail."

Clearly the two partners had become so symbiotic that it was no longer possible for even Purcell to distinguish his own design. The Hoyt House may be the definitive example of Purcell and Elmslie's unique ability to dovetail their diverse talents to achieve the ultimate expression of architectural genius.

TALL TALE

"One can see how I was always yearning for buildings with tall steep roofs and turned to that form whenever the occasion offered," said Purcell years later when looking back on his design for the Adair House. For this commission the client, Dr. John H. Adair, rejected Elmslie's elegant low-slung Prairie-style house as too expensive. Purcell then leaped at his chance to raise the roof and called on his talented draftswoman, Marion Parker, to help. "George was in Chicago and unavailable for the necessary conference of restudy, so Miss Parker and I got busy on the project and developed a wholly new design," Purcell recalled. Elmslie later added decorative embellishments to the house.

Purcell and Elmslie were introduced to Adair by Charles Buxton, whose own Prairie-style bungalow was just a few blocks away (page 104). Both indirectly owed their homes' designs to Carl K. Bennett of the National Farmers' Bank. The Owatonna banker opened doors to as many as ten commissions for the architects, including the Adair and Buxton residences.

Purcell prided himself on his sensitivity to the needs of the housewife. When it came time to revise the design of the Adairs' home, he carefully considered Mary Adair's concerns.

"Aside from any question of what you think it wise to invest in a house," Purcell wrote to Dr. Adair, "there is . . . the housework question. Such a house in Minneapolis is one thing—it is quite another matter to keep it in the order I am sure Mrs. Adair would insist upon in Owatonna." Still, this large house must have posed a challenge.

Outwardly the Adair House has much in common with Frank Lloyd Wright's Hills-DeCaro House (1906) in Oak Park, Illinois. Both are three stories with imposing stepped-back hipped roofs and attic bedrooms. Wright soon left the attic behind to bring his houses closer to the ground, but Purcell liked the high roof and tucked two bedrooms beneath the steep pitch forming the third story. The second floor holds three more sleeping quarters.

The Adair House is essentially a straightforward cube set beneath a tall, hipped roof that steps back eleven times until it reaches the apex (above). Original specifications suggested that the lapped redwood siding be treated with oil and left unstained. Natural materials treated naturally was a hallmark of the Prairie style and the Arts and Crafts movement. A band of stucco marks the second story.

A one-story wing branches out at right to hold the entrance and the sun porch (opposite). Tiny blue diamonds in sawn wood around the doorway echo the shape and color of art glass inside.

A window seat hides the radiator beneath the front window (left). On the far wall, built-in art glass cabinets stretch the room's full width to provide plentiful storage. The glass is patterned with deep blue diamonds—one diamond in each glass panel—a motif repeated in the dining room breakfront. This diamond pattern echoes the exterior fret-sawn wood ornament, relating the house's design inside and out.

The entrance to the 2,900-square-foot house is positioned asymmetrically on the right, allowing the living room to spread across the front facade. Inside, the generous rooms are elegantly appointed. Built-in furnishings, art glass, and Elmslie's unifying diamond motif tie the plan together. Double wood banding wraps around walls and skims the ceiling to emphasize the horizontality of the prairie. A glass-enclosed veranda off the front hallway pushes the house's boundaries out of its cube.

Elmslie's arched fireplace offers a graceful contrast to the living room's rectilinear lines. Mary Adair at first rejected the design, but Purcell urged her to reconsider: "Square openings have been done to death," he wrote her. "As we have it, with the tiny rainbow of glass mosaic—something like the blue and gold glass found in the bank—it is so charming." Fortunately, she relented. She died shortly after the house was finished, but Dr. Adair and his daughters remained in the house for several more years. Decades later, Purcell had fond memories of Dr. Adair: "I like to think of this genial and sincere M.D. and his two daughters keeping house for him."

The home's current owners, James P. Sandberg and Ruth Makinen, tolerated a seventy-mile one-way commute to Minneapolis for five years just to own this piece of Owatonna history. "Our jaws dropped when we saw the interior of the house the first time," Sandberg recalls. "We had already studied the blueprints at the Northwest Architectural Archives, but we didn't expect the interior to have survived as well as it has." The couple make full use of the large home, using the attic bedrooms as work spaces. But their favorite spot is the enclosed "family porch," where tall casement windows allow them to enjoy the delights every season has to offer.

"I was so pleased when Mr. Elmslie thought of this dainty arch form," Purcell said of the fireplace (below). Surrounded by a "rainbow of glass mosaic," as he described it, the semicircular fan of brick on a raised hearth is the focus of the living room. The dominant colors are blue and gold, similar to the glass colors on Louis Sullivan's National Farmers' Bank (1906) in downtown Owatonna.

The dining room, adjacent to the living room, is accessed through a pair of French doors with frosted glass in a simple linear design reminiscent of a Japanese shoji screen (opposite). For light fixtures in both rooms, Elmslie turned to a familiar motif: a circle in a square. The lights are operated by a wall switch, but a delicately braided narrow rope culminating in a tiny carved wooden acorn once controlled a dimming mechanism, according to the current owners. Only one of these remains, on the dining room fixture.

When the French doors are open, space unfolds unhindered from the living room to the entrance to the porch (below). A smaller hanging fixture lights the entrance. A screen of square spindles hides the stairway from view.

Fresh Start

"Mrs. Bradley really had the house-building fever," recalled Purcell. In just seven years, Josephine Crane Bradley built three major Prairie-style houses, all financed by her wealthy father, Charles R. Crane, who also commissioned a dozen smaller structures from Purcell and Elmslie over the years. No wonder Purcell called Crane "our best client."

Josephine's first Prairie house, a wedding gift from her father, was designed in 1909 by Louis Sullivan with Elmslie's assistance. Although beautiful, the richly detailed house in Madison, Wisconsin, was too large and extravagant for Josephine and her university professor husband, Harold Bradley, and they sold it at a loss after only a few years. Sullivan's rare venture into residential design failed, Purcell explained later, because his "knowledge and experience in family living and housekeeping . . . was, in truth[,] nearly zero."

One bright spot emerged from the endeavor. Josephine worked closely with Elmslie, who, unlike his sometimes volatile employer, actually listened to her requests. In 1911, after a falling out with Sullivan, Josephine and her father chose Elmslie to design a seaside bungalow on Cape Cod (page 92) and then a new house in Madison. By this time Elmslie had left Sullivan's office and was working with Purcell and Feick in Minneapolis. Elmslie brought several other wealthy but exasperated Sullivan clients to the firm, including Carl K. Bennett and Henry Babson.

Josephine and Elmslie worked together like "an ideal pair," Harold Bradley recalled in 1965. Elmslie was "highly perceptive, and would come back later with what we thought were ideal solutions and arrangements.... We three became warm friends in the process." Elmslie's new plan could not have been more different from Sullivan's dark, brooding, impractical design. Filled with light and the latest conveniences, it was the "perfect machine for accomplishing . . . household life as automatically as possible," Purcell recounted. "The closets and store-rooms were a maze of specialized subdivisions for every possible article. The kitchen was a pioneer study in scientific arrangement."

Composed of creamy stucco over red brick, the Bradley House rises three stories on the street side but just two in the rear toward Lake Mendota. Wood trim rhythmically outlines walls and windows, stressing the horizontal line of the prairie. Open terraces and porches reach out from the house like platters. A low hipped roof floats on ribbons of windows that hug overhanging eaves in the best Prairie tradition. Crisp and linear, Elmslie's modern design for the Bradleys forecast streamlined houses decades into the future.

One of the firm's most sophisticated designs, the pared-down Bradley House was a portent of things to come (left). The sheltering roofs, bands of windows, and sweeping lines epitomize the Prairie style at its maturity. Although three stories, it maintains a horizontal feel. The main living space was on the second floor; the upper story held the bedrooms, while the lower level was reserved for the playroom and the garage. Piers of dark red brick frame the lower-level entrance (right). Hiding in a niche is a small sample of Elmslie's signature sawn-wood ornament.

Elmslie cleverly incorporated a monogram to personalize the front door (opposite, top left), merging the two family names with a *B* for Bradley and a *C* for Crane. The front door opens into a vestibule (opposite, top center) leading up to the main living space on the second floor. A life-size portrait of Josephine Crane Bradley painted by the famed Czech artist Alphonse Mucha once held the prominent spot on the far wall. A built-in garage behind the left wall was converted into a workshop when the new garage was added in the 1920s. The children's playroom is to the right. The entry settle is by L. & J. G. Stickley. From the living room, space unfolds naturally through an intimate hallway beyond the fireplace (opposite, top right). Art glass–enclosed bookcases and a small window covered in fret-sawn wood make this narrow vestibule far more than a transitional area. An antique white alabaster statue of St. Anthony of Padua graces one bookcase.

The main entrance, located between brick piers on the lower level, opens into the first floor, where Elmslie created a playroom for the Bradleys' seven sons and a built-in garage. Near the staircase to the second floor, the architect carved out a prime location for a nearly life-size portrait of Josephine commissioned in 1909 from the renowned Czechoslovakian artist Alphonse Mucha, whose romantic work came to define the Art Nouveau style. Ten years later, when the Czech government approached Mucha for a design to grace the one hundred–crown banknote, he offered his flowing portrait of Josephine in a tree, and this Czech banknote remained in circulation until World War II.

As in many of Wright's Prairie houses, life in the Bradley House took place mainly on the second floor. Here a large living room opens onto a sun porch that stretches into the treetops. Fixed glass on the eastern end allows distant views of Lake Mendota below, while casement windows on either side bring in refreshing breezes. Windows on three sides fill the room with "gorgeous light," say the current owners. A generous Roman brick fireplace with the trademark raised hearth marks the transition between living and dining spaces, which are accessed by a wide vestibule. The dining room, large enough for a family of nine, is also suffused with light. Built-in cabinets open directly into the butler's pantry. A small breakfast porch offers glimpses of the lake below.

Hanging lights of brushed silver with half-moon glass shades glow in the four corners of the living room (right). South-facing windows bring in natural light all day long, especially in the cold Wisconsin winters when the sun traces a low path in the sky. "We find the house to be incredibly livable," say the current owners. Their L. & J. G. Stickley furnishings in quarter-sawn white oak with a Craftsman finish suit the room perfectly. The Bradley House's main spaces pivot around the central fireplace, with its comforting raised hearth. The receiving hall is accessed through the wide opening on the right. The dining room, directly behind the fireplace, unfolds from a transitional space lined in bookcases on the left. Original drawings indicate that the fireplace was planned to open into both the living and dining rooms. French doors that look south lead from the dining room to a breakfast porch (below), a wonderful spot to soak in the sun's warmth and enjoy alfresco meals. Distant views of Lake Mendota are possible when the leaves have fallen.

The Bradleys filled the dining room with a large round table and enough chairs for themselves and their seven sons (above). The current owners chose an antique mahogany table, also round, with lion feet and acanthus knees ringed by matching handcarved Chippendale chairs. The lowered ceiling in the wide hallway leading to the living room compresses the space and "makes you want to step into the next room," they say.

The butler's pantry (right) was remodeled when a new kitchen and breakfast room with a fireplace were created. For the three-part illuminated skylight added above the new fireplace (page 8), the owners enlarged Elmslie's sawn-wood design in the front doorway niche. From the pantry, sliding doors permitted the Bradleys' maid to access the dining room buffet (below left). This and other original woodwork has never been painted. A large diamond-paned art glass door from the Hoyt House (page 149), removed during a remodeling, graces the new kitchen suite (below right). For the adjacent cabinets, the owners had to assemble the art glass themselves.

The original kitchen and the maid's bedroom and her living room have been transformed into a large kitchen, using the built-in pantry cabinets as a design template. The owners scoured the country for just the right materials to suit the room's 1914 aesthetic. Replicating Elmslie's original design for a new fireplace (page 8) led them to an obscure brick factory in Kansas that makes the narrow Roman brick, favored by Prairie architects, just once every five years. "We bought it all," they note. The limestone hearth came from the same Mankato, Minnesota, quarry as the original. In Plymouth, Wisconsin, they located a company with the formula for the iridescent Prairie-style art glass they were seeking; in Chicago they found the narrow leading to connect the glass pieces. They were unable, however, to find anyone to make the art glass windows to suit their exacting standards. "We made them ourselves," they relate. "We had to."

A powder room and an office for Harold Bradley fill out the rest of the second story. Working closely with Josephine, Elmslie outfitted her husband's office with everything necessary for a hard-working university professor: a built-in desk, a card catalogue, a file cabinet, and even a built-in chair with a view of the lake. Bradley was a beloved figure on the University of Wisconsin campus, where he met his future wife before 1907. She was a wealthy heiress, and he was "one of the wildest characters I've ever bumped into," his eldest son, Charles, wrote in 1983. "If he couldn't find adventure, he made it."

Son of the Sierra Club cofounder Cornelius Beach Bradley and an avid outdoorsman, Harold Bradley taught all of his boys how to swim, skate, dance, ski, and play baseball and tennis. They were primed for camping trips by sleeping outside on the house's open porches—even in the winter. Bradley erected a ski jump and taught all the local children how to use it. He built a concrete tennis court, Wisconsin's first, behind his house.

In the garage at the lowest level of the house, Bradley kept a motorcycle, which he rode to work, summer and winter. When the snow was too deep, he skied. In the 1920s the small garage was turned into a workshop and a larger garage with servants' quarters was added to the original house. Although not designed by Purcell and Elmslie, it balances the original design.

Harold Bradley's study was a model of efficiency and comfort (above). Mint green fabric, slightly worn but still original, covers a built-in chair, with a reading light overhead and a window to look out. Card catalogues and file cabinets, also built in, kept the professor's records close at hand.

All of the bedrooms have art glass windows and southern exposures for maximum sunlight. Corner windows make a guest room, furnished with a Stickley bed, feel like it sits in a tree house (opposite). In another guest room with twin Stickley beds made of oak, a simple brick fireplace offers welcoming warmth (above).

The third floor holds four bedrooms, two sleeping porches, two bathrooms, and a small balcony. Deaf since childhood, Josephine had learned to read lips quite proficiently but asked Elmslie to put clear glass in the bedroom doors so she could keep an eye on her boys. Because of her deafness, she was also deeply afraid of fire; every floor in the house is outfitted with a large canvas fire hose tucked into specially designed cabinets.

Looking back on this design, Purcell remarked that the house "was far in advance of its time, with the result that today it takes its place as a distinctly contemporary building amongst later dwellings which have long ago become dated." Josephine Bradley liked the up-to-date conveniences but wondered if her new home was not too modern. "Well, it's a lovely house and we like it, but perhaps we did overdo the machinery a little bit. Sometimes it feels a bit like living in some kind of glorified office building," she told Purcell. It was nonetheless the perfect dwelling for a remarkable family. Elmslie's sensitive and imaginative design spelled home to a fun-loving professor, his beautiful heiress wife, and their seven rambunctious boys.

The canvas fire hose in the second-floor hall cupboard is still operable (above right); wood for the fireplace is stored beneath. The upstairs guest bath (below left) and the powder room (below right) retain their original Crane plumbing (Josephine Bradley's father's family owned the Crane Plumbing Company).

PERFECT HARMONY

Charles Backus was a piano tuner with grand ideas. On one of his twice-yearly visits to tune Purcell's piano, he asked if the architect could design for him an inexpensive house with the same beauty and grace as Purcell's own home on Lake Place. Purcell thought he could. Backus and his wife, Adeline, then presented Purcell with a list of ideas that challenged the architect to come up with a low-cost yet beautiful Prairie house. "These ideas interested Mr. Purcell," the Backuses' daughter Marion recalled in 1967, "and that was the reason, I think, why he offered to take on the job of building the house."

The Backuses, according to their daughter, did not want a front porch because it would keep out the sun. The living room and dining room, they suggested, should be treated as one space but offer privacy from the front door when the family was at dinner. They wanted a breakfast nook in the kitchen, and on the second floor they needed a cool room for sleeping and a warm room in which to dress.

It was a tall order, but Purcell and Elmslie delivered on each request. The result was a Prairie-style masterpiece on a proletarian budget. When asked why he bothered with such a modest project, Purcell replied: "The large ones, we build for money, but this, I want to build for fun." The 1,200-square-foot house cost about $3,000 in 1915. Purcell joked that he made a profit of only $4.05.

Measuring twenty-five by twenty-seven feet, the house is a classic Prairie foursquare with grouped casement windows, a low hipped roof with wide overhangs, strong horizontal lines, and an asymmetrical entrance. Purcell called it a "simple little house with a big meaning," one that featured "a lot of pioneer thinking." Purcell and Elmslie's first design featured a tall, peaked roof, but the Backuses rejected that plan because they wanted the house to look more like Purcell's own home.

In one of the best of Purcell and Elmslie's open plans, space flows seamlessly from the foyer through the living room and around the spindled screen shielding the dining room (right). Windows above cabinets accentuate the horizontal line. There was no money for ornament, but it was not missed in the uncluttered, elegant spaces.

Trellis-topped pillars announce the entrance to the only Purcell and Elmslie house in Minneapolis that retains its original coloring (below left). The low budget inspired the multipurpose wall of bookcases and cupboards that serviced "meals at one end through books to music, etc. at the other," as Purcell wrote (below right).

The spindled screen hides both the dining room and the hallway leading upstairs (above left). The stairway was placed at the center of the house, making it easy to reach from any area downstairs. The Backus House, in meticulous condition, retains its original clawfoot tub and toilet tank made of oak lined with copper in the upstairs bathroom (above right). A wall of cabinets, out of view, provides ample storage.

Although small, the house is one of the firm's most functional and comfortable. Except for the kitchen, the first floor is treated as one large room with only a partial screen of square oak spindles separating living and dining spaces. This is one of the few houses Purcell and Elmslie designed without a fireplace, allowing the spindled screen to divide the space much as fireplaces do in their other designs. The effect is one of remarkable spaciousness.

The home's focal point is a wall of built-in oak cabinets that stretch the full twenty-five-foot width of the dining and living rooms. When shown a photograph of the cabinets in 1939, Purcell called them "astonishingly modern, anticipating decorative forms that have only recently appeared in New York penthouses." Space was provided here for dishes, linens, sheet music, and books. A high ribbon of windows runs atop the shelves, bringing light into the room while providing privacy.

Upstairs, Purcell made good on his promise of a cool room for sleeping and a warm room for dressing. He combined a large bedroom with a smaller one to create a master suite, with oak folding doors to shut off the small room so it could be heated separately. A second bedroom and a bathroom with an entire wall of cabinets fill out the rest of the upstairs.

As far as Rolf Anderson, the current owner, is concerned, the house is Purcell and Elmslie's best small open plan. He should know. Formerly president of the Minnesota Chapter of the Society of Architectural Historians and the Preservation Alliance of Minnesota, he has spent a great deal of time studying historic architecture. This is where Anderson has always wanted to live. He praises the Backuses for their courage in commissioning such an unconventional house. "We respect the work of architects, but it takes a client to get something like this built," he says. "It's always fascinating when people are willing to build a house that doesn't look like everyone else's."

Purcell and Elmslie created a master suite at the front of the house (right). The transition between its rooms is marked by a low soffit and oak folding doors that help retain heat. A band of windows seems to enlarge the space. The current owner uses the smaller bedroom as a study. The lamp next to the bed is a Wright reproduction.

Mountain Reverie

Ideas gleaned from the prairie translated into a different form when Purcell designed a house for Louis Heitman in a broad Montana valley within view of mountains. "The gallant rise of steep roofs into tall wedges always fascinated me and I was eager to do houses with this mass," Purcell later remarked. With Elmslie occupied in Chicago with other work, Purcell composed a tall, peaked house that reflected the mountains instead of the prairie. He took it as a matter of great pride when told in 1935 that Montana's state architect described the house as "the most contemporary and desirable dwelling in the city."

A German immigrant, Heitman traveled west with his wife in the late 1800s to seek his fortune in gold, according to Purcell. His destination was Montana. Whether he found gold or not is unknown, but he did find prosperity. By the time he commissioned a new house in Helena, he had risen to become president of the American National Bank and a leading citizen. At a 1911 family reunion in Minneapolis, Heitman was introduced to the work of Purcell and Elmslie by a relative, John Leuthold, who was planning a house for his daughter (page 106). Purcell recalled that when they met, Heitman "was all fired up to build himself a home and build it quick. He had no conception of how long it took to plan a house and make the working drawings. I realized that he would never be patient to go through with the process."

Like the parsonage of Purcell and Elmslie's First Congregational Church (1913) in Eau Claire, Wisconsin, the Heitman House's steep gables have no projecting eaves, giving it a stark, bold look (opposite). In contrast, a trellis-covered porch provides a comforting sense of shelter at the entrance.

Purcell was pleased when the residence's second owner, J. E. O'Connell, informed him that the house had survived several severe earthquakes and hundreds of aftershocks that had seriously damaged almost every other building in Helena in 1935. The architect attributed this feat to the wedge-shaped roof and its "tremendous triangulated bracing" (below).

PHOTOGRAPH BY SCOT ZIMMERMAN

It took some time, but eventually Heitman did build a house. The first scheme in 1911 was rejected as too lavish and expensive, as was a revision. In 1916 the Heitmans finally settled on a design with a steeply pitched roof, integrated furnishings, and a spacious interior. "They liked it in every way," Purcell recalled, but noted with irony: "As often happens, the final project as built was more elaborate and cost more money than the two earlier projects that were laid aside as 'too expensive.'"

In selecting building materials, Purcell looked back to his sojourns in California in 1905, when he observed the highly personalized Arts and Crafts houses of Bernard Maybeck. "I had always remembered the distinguished use of broad simple wood panels by Maybeck around Berkeley," he wrote, "so I sent to California and had special redwood panels 24 inches wide sawn and crated to Helena." The wide boards set into the steep gables with no overhang hint at the English revival styles that influenced the Arts and Crafts movement. Originally the panels were stained brown to highlight the wood's natural qualities and give the house a more rustic appearance.

Purcell considered the Heitman House a "pioneer demonstration" in the use of wood. Like Wright, he treated all natural materials with great respect. Conventional architects failed to understand wood's unique qualities, Purcell said. "Worse, designers asked wood to imitate stone [and] put it to other unworthy uses."

The floor plan of the 5,000-square-foot residence is unusual for the firm. Here the maid's room, kitchen, entrance, and sunroom are lined up across the facade, with the dining room, study, and living room at the back. The living and dining rooms do not flow together as they do in most Purcell and Elmslie houses but are separated by the study. More typical is the second floor, holding a sewing room, a master bedroom, two smaller bedrooms, a sleeping porch, and a bathroom. On the third floor are two more bedrooms, a twelve-foot cedar closet, and another bathroom.

Purcell experimented with a back-to-back fireplace opening into the living room and the library, but the result was only marginally successful. "The fireplace drew perfectly as long as no one opened any doors and if the curtains in the opening between the living room and library were not closed," Purcell wrote. All of the built-in and freestanding furniture pieces were built by Harry Rubins of the John S. Bradstreet Company of Minneapolis.

Outfitted with the latest conveniences, the Heitman House was the model of modernity. It had an electric washing machine, a vacuum cleaner system accessible in every room, and an Edison phonograph built into a cabinet that served both the living room and the sun porch; a burglar system, controlled by a master switch at the head of Mrs. Heitman's bed, turned on one light in every room and at all outside entrances.

The Heitmans both died around 1930 and the house passed to J. E. O'Connell, who operated Eddy's Bakery in Helena. O'Connell kept in touch with Purcell, even sending him a fruitcake at the sanitarium where the architect was being treated for tuberculosis. "I am ready to write you a testimonial," Purcell wrote in thanks. "'Having eaten three of your well-known mountain fruit cakes, I am now a complete cure.' Yes, sir, Mr. O'Connell, these t.b. bugs seem to be subdued."

O'Connell's son, James, and his wife, Murel, have lived in the house since 1973 and raised six children here. "We really filled the house up," Murel notes with a laugh.

The living room's focal point is a dramatic arched fireplace (left), which is inset with a mural featuring steep-roofed buildings recalling Heitman's homeland. In lieu of a mantel, a wide slash of polychrome terra cotta carries a raised pattern.

THE SIMPLE LIFE

"Fritz Carlson was a warm hearted young Swedish foreman, an excellent craftsman with an orderly and logical mind," Purcell recalled. Like the tinsmith Ed Goetzenberger, Carlson was one of those "common men" of the building trades regarded by Purcell as among his "warmest friends." Carlson worked on several Purcell and Elmslie buildings, including banks in Hector and Madison, Minnesota. When he was about to be married, he told Purcell that he wanted to build "a little house for himself," Purcell recalled. "He would not live in anything that we had not designed, so I told him he could pay us $100 and charge up the rest of the architect's fees to a wedding present."

Purcell pulled out a familiar design from the firm's repertoire and then simplified it to suit Carlson's needs and budget. "My idea was to reduce this whole program to its minimum plan for decent comfort and minimum materials," Purcell wrote. Like the Goetzenberger (page 67) and Hineline (page 76) houses, the two-story Carlson residence has an open plan with a high gabled roof and several porches projecting off its rectangular form. The first-floor space flows easily from entrance to living room to dining room around the central fireplace situated at the house's center. Upstairs are three bedrooms, a bathroom, and a sleeping porch. Like so many of the firm's smaller, low-cost dwellings, this wood-and-stucco house is an excellent example of Purcell and Elmslie's ability to open up a floor plan and unite interior and exterior spaces.

Charlie Koch and Kathy Holm, the fourth and present owners, found that some features had been altered or removed after Carlson left in 1960. The fireplace, for one, had lost its L-shaped notch, making the opening appear to be asymmetrical. Koch became obsessed with setting things right. He visited the Purcell-Cutts House, interviewed the Carlsons' nephew, and talked to preservationists to help him decide what to do. Yet overall the house had retained its integrity, including a commanding breakfront in the dining room.

After Purcell relocated to Portland, Oregon, in 1919, he tried to interest a developer in a housing development based on the Carlson House, commissioning a beautiful color rendering (pages 46–47) to sell the idea. But the real estate business in Portland during the 1920s was, as the architect ruefully observed, "filled with shoddy, high-pressure building and selling campaigns." The project unfortunately went unbuilt.

For the living area the current owners commissioned new art glass panels based on a 1922 Elmslie design (below left). They added a square spindled screen to conceal the entrance (below right). Purcell and Elmslie lavished the same attention on this small workingman's house (opposite) as they did on larger commissions.

Good Bones

When Kim and Tim Taylor relocated to Minneapolis from California in 1994, they had just five days to find a house to buy. "We looked at seventy-five houses in the suburbs and the city," including the Wiethoff House, Tim recalls. Frustrated and unable to agree, they decided to each name his and her top house. For Tim, this Purcell and Elmslie residence was number one. For Kim it was seventy-one. "We had a heart-to-heart spousal moment," Tim says, but he finally won her over.

Kim loves the house now, although her reservations are easy to understand given her description of its condition. In a seller's market the home had been for sale for three months. Owned by a bachelor, "it hadn't been cleared out in years," she notes. The hedge outside was so overgrown that it completely covered the front and side windows. "It was taller than the front door" and had caused the front porch to rot, she relates.

Today the house is pristine, open, and airy. The hedge has been removed, allowing the large windows to fill the house with natural light. "Purcell and Elmslie oriented the house to the light," Tim explains. The architects also took advantage of the odd-shaped lot to create extra privacy. "The house is angled slightly," Tim notes, so the side windows look into the neighbors' yard, not their house. The central front window was originally leaded in diamond shapes for additional privacy but was changed to plate glass by a previous owner.

A number of clever techniques made this and other modest Purcell and Elmslie houses seem more spacious and refined than larger revival-style houses of the day. The living room flows seamlessly into the dining area, divided only by an L-shaped wall holding a built-in cabinet that opens directly into the dining room. More storage is found in the four-part black walnut closet embedded in the staircase at the front entrance; a lower section forms another L-shaped partition to screen the staircase while keeping the space open. "It's a very contemporary house in terms of flow," Kim observes. "Nobody can believe it was built in 1917."

Purcell and Elmslie's clients were Charles and Meta Wiethoff, a doctor and his wife. They lived here with their son and a maid, who could be summoned with a tap of the foot on the call button under the dining table. Her domain was the basement, but that wasn't all bad. "The basement has nine-foot ceilings and large egress windows," Tim explains. The maid's coat closet was tucked into the kitchen, and she had her own room upstairs with a stained glass window, a Murphy bed, and a sink. Three additional bedrooms are found upstairs, all with simple tulip-patterned art glass windows.

The Taylors hired a local designer, Kelly Marshall, to create a new Arts and Crafts-style rug for the living room. She made a similar one for Joan and Walter Mondale, the former U.S. vice president who is a Minneapolis resident. "The rug is now known as 'the Mondale rug,'" Kim says. "That has more cachet than 'the Taylor rug.'" The couple also removed decades of wallpaper, using some of the restorers responsible for work on the Purcell-Cutts House. They have more plans for their home, but for now they feel settled. Kim Taylor has never regretted being talked into buying the house. "Tim was right," she admits. "The house has good bones."

The bold arched fireplace encircled in brick and wood is "like the sun rising," Kim Taylor says (opposite). Its L-shaped notch holds a cabinet that opens onto the dining room. Lapped cedar siding rises up to meet second-story windows placed in stucco (above). The roofline projects eight feet from the walls, shading the windows.

Three windows grouped below and two above, out of view, light the stairway to the second story (below). Four built-in storage cabinets made of black walnut shield the stairs from the living room and provide storage in a convenient place. One cabinet is smaller, giving the unit the same L-shaped composition as the fireplace wall.

The built-in breakfront was designed with ultimate care—even the drawer handles are decorated (above left). The mirror helps reflect light into the dining room. A door on the right leads to the kitchen.

Seventeen windows, including one in a small space serving as a child's closet (opposite), feature an elegant tulip design. Most are on the second story, which holds four bedrooms and a bath. More subtle and linear than some of Elmslie's other designs, the windows suit the Wiethoff House's contemporary feel. While windows in the stair hall have a touch of orange, upstairs they include shades of pale blue, yellow, and green.

The Work of Purcell and Elmslie

The following list highlights some of the more than four hundred commissions and projects designed by Purcell and Elmslie from 1907 to 1921. Before George Elmslie joined the firm in 1910, William Gray Purcell practiced alone with George Feick (1907–1909), and for about two years afterward the firm was named Purcell, Feick and Elmslie (1910–13); it then became Purcell and Elmslie (1913–21). The firm's work includes about 120 residential designs (around 50 of them unbuilt projects), some 40 residential alterations, 23 banks (13 of them projects), 45 commercial designs (29 projects), 12 civic structures (8 projects), 6 school buildings (5 projects), and 17 religious structures (11 projects). In addition, the partners produced residential outbuildings and landscaping, furnishings, and graphic designs (publications and exhibits). Unbuilt projects are indicated below by italics. At the end of each entry is the commission number: P&F indicates Purcell and Feick; PF&E indicates Purcell, Feick and Elmslie; and P&E indicates Purcell and Elmslie.

Residences

1907 Catherine Gray House, Minneapolis, P&F no. 5

1907 *Truman B. Taylor House, project, Sandusky, Ohio, P&F no. 7*

1907 *W. J. Landon Duplex House, project, Winona, Minn., P&F no. 9*

1908 Fred Larson House, Towner, N.D., P&F no. 11

1908 *F. W. Bird Company House competition, P&F no. 15*

1908 *John H. Kahler House, project, Rochester, Minn., P&F no. 18A*

1908 Arthur Jones House, barn alteration, Minneapolis, P&F no. 23

1908 *Ladies' Home Journal Cottage design, P&F no. 25*

1908 George Feick Sr. Houses, Sandusky, Ohio, P&F no. 32

1908 H. J. Myers House, Minneapolis, P&F no. 33

1908 O. A. Pierce House, Lake Minnetonka, Minn., P&F no. 36

1909 Mrs. Terrance McCosker House, Minneapolis, P&F no. 40

1909 J.D.R. Steven Cottage, Eau Claire, Wis., P&F no. 47

1909 J.D.R. Steven House, Eau Claire, Wis., P&F no. 48

1909 E. M. Thompson House, Bismarck, N.D., P&F no. 49

1909 Charles A. Purcell House, River Forest, Ill., P&F no. 51

1909 Theodore H. Beaulieu House, White Earth, Minn., P&F no. 53

1909 Henry G. Goosman House, Minneapolis, P&F no. 60

1909 H. P. Gallaher House, Lake Minnetonka, Minn., P&F no. 62

1909 *E. C. Warner House, project, Minneapolis, P&F no. 63*

1909 Patrick Byrne House, Bismarck, N.D., PF&E no. 69

1910 *Harry Blair Duplex Houses, project, Winona, Minn., PF&E no. 72*

1910 Edward Goetzenberger House, Minneapolis, PF&E no. 77

1910 *George Stricker House, project, Minneapolis, PF&E no. 79*

1910 T. R. Atkinson House, Bismarck, N.D., PF&E no. 81

1910 S. F. Blymyer Cottage no. 1, Lake Minnetonka, Minn., PF&E no. 82

1910 A.B.C. Dodd House, Charles City, Iowa, PF&E no. 83

1910 *C. F. Clark House, project, Cedar Rapids, Iowa, PF&E no. 84*

1910 Josephine Crane Bradley House no. 1, Madison, Wis., PF&E no. 89*

1910 James B. Thompson Cabin, northern Minn., PF&E no. 92

1910 Charles W. Sexton House, major alteration, Minnetonka, Minn., PF&E no. 94

1910 E. L. Powers House, Minneapolis, PF&E no. 98

1910 Harold Hineline House, Minneapolis, PF&E no. 102

1911 *S. F. Blymyer Summer House no. 2, project, Lake Minnetonka, Minn., PF&E no. 109*

1911 Lyman E. Wakefield House, Minneapolis, PF&E no. 111

1911 E. A. Knowlton House, Rochester, Minn., PF&E no. 116

1911 Carlo Jorgenson House, Bismarck, N.D., PF&E no. 120

1911 *Mrs. B. T. McIndoe House, project, Rhinelander, Wis., PF&E no. 121*

1911 *Louis E. Heitman House, first scheme, project, Helena, Mont., PF&E no. 122*

1911 *Henry J. Weber House, project, Austin, Minn., PF&E no. 123*

1911 Crane Estate Gardener's Cottage, Woods Hole, Mass., PF&E no. 127

1911 Dr. Oscar Owre House, Minneapolis, PF&E no. 130

1911 Charles R. Crane (Bradley) Summer Bungalow, Woods Hole, Mass., PF&E no. 131

1911 *Henry W. Benton House, project, Wayzata, Minn., PF&E no. 134*

1911 *Henry Babson speculative houses, project, Riverside, Ill., PF&E no. 136*

1912 *H. S. Adams House, project, Oak Park, Ill., PF&E no. 139*

1912 *Dr. W. F. Braasch House, project, Rochester, Minn., PF&E no. 145*

1912 Crane Estate Four Cottages, Woods Hole, Mass., PF&E no. 147

1912 Charles Crane Buzzard's Bay Cottages, Woods Hole, Mass., PF&E no. 149

1912 *Dr. A. D. Daniels House, project, Rhinelander, Wis., PF&E no. 150*

1912 *E. Frank Hussey House, project, Minneapolis, PF&E no. 151*

1912 Mrs. C. I. Buxton Bungalow, Owatonna, Minn., PF&E no. 154

1912 John Leuthold (Beebe) House, St. Paul, Minn., PF&E no. 155

1912 E. C. Tillotson House, Minneapolis, PF&E no. 157

1912 *Henry D. Page House, project, Mason City, Iowa, PF&E no. 159*

1912 *E. W. Decker House, first scheme, Lake Minnetonka, Minn., PF&E no. 167*

1912 Lockwood Summer Home, Hayward, Wis., PF&E no. 171

1912 John S. Owen Cottage, location unknown, PF&E no. 173

1912 Maurice Wolf House, Minneapolis, PF&E no. 174

1912 *J. E. Meyers House, project, Minneapolis, PF&E no. 178*

1912 Charles Parker House, Minneapolis, PF&E no. 179

1913 Dr. J.W.S. Gallagher House, Winona, Minn., PF&E no. 187

*A Louis Sullivan commission, but Elmslie finished the interior work under Purcell, Feick and Elmslie when he left Sullivan's office.

Banks

Commercial Structures

1907 Motor Inn for Henry Goosman, Minneapolis, P&F no. 3

1907 Butler Brothers fireworks warehouse, Minneapolis, P&F no. 4

1907 *Singer Building for I. P. Baker, project, Bismarck, N.D., P&F no. 17*

1907 *Elks Club, project, Mankato, Minn., P&F no. 27*

1907 Reel and Rudder Club, Lake Minnetonka, Minn., P&F no. 28

1907 *Shakopee Sanitarium, project, Shakopee, Minn., P&F no. 37*

1908 George Feick Sr. office building, Sandusky, Ohio, P&F no. 41

1908 *Sears E. Brace Jr. and Company warehouse, project, Minneapolis, P&F no. 42*

1908 *Carlyle Scott commercial building, project, Minneapolis, P&F no. 52*

1909 Dayton Company fitting rooms, Minneapolis, P&F no. 57

1910 Electric Carriage and Battery Company garage, Minneapolis, PF&E no. 74

1910 *Elks Club, project, Winona, Minn., PF&E no. 100*

1910 Paul Mueller Studio, Minneapolis, PF&E no. 104

1911 *Dayton's Dry Goods Company tea rooms, project, Minneapolis, PF&E no. 117*

1911 *Frank H. Blackmaar Sanitarium, project, Chicago, PF&E no. 118*

1911 Clayton F. Summy Music Store, salesroom, Chicago, PF&E no. 135

1912 *Eaton, Crane and Pike offices, project, Chicago, PF&E no. 140*

1912 *Interstate Mercantile Company, project, Winona, Minn., PF&E no. 156*

1912 Edison Shop office building, Chicago, PF&E no. 170

1912 *Chippewa Valley Light and Power, project, Eau Claire, Wis., PF&E no. 180*

1913 *Women's Club Auditorium, project, Minneapolis, PF&E no. 208*

1913 *Clayton F. Summy Music Store, project, Chicago, PF&E no. 211*

1914 *Riverside Country Club, project, Riverside, Ill., P&E no. 235*

1914 Edison Shop office building, San Francisco, Calif., P&E no. 242

1914 *Gusto Cigarette Company, project, Minneapolis, P&E no. 254*

1914 Minnesota Phonograph Company store, Minneapolis, P&E no. 258

1915 *Rhinelander Hotel "Welcome Inn," project, Rhinelander, Wis., P&E no. 268*

1915 F. N. Hegg commercial building, Minneapolis, P&E no. 296

1916 Northwest Lumber land office building, Stanley, Wis., P&E no. 320

1917 James Wallace commercial building, Minneapolis, P&E no. 334

1917 *George E. Logan store, project, Mitchell, S.D., P&E no. 337*

1917 International Leather and Belting factory, Chicago, P&E no. 340A

1917 International Leather and Belting factory, New Haven, Conn., P&E no. 340B

1917 *International Leather and Belting factory, project, Cleveland, Ohio, P&E no. 340C*

1917 *International Leather and Belting garage, project, unknown, P&E no. 340D*

1917 *Biddle Store, project, Philadelphia, Pa., P&E no. 341*

1917 *MacPhail Studios music school, project, Minneapolis, P&E no. 346*

1918 *C. L. Atwood Store, project, St. Cloud, Minn., P&E no. 352*

1918 *C. L. Atwood Hotel, project, St. Cloud, Minn., P&E no. 355*

1918 *Riverside Country Club, project, second scheme, Riverside, Ill., P&E no. 379*

1918 *Charlotte Leather Belting Company factory, project, Charlotte, N.C., P&E no. 380*

1919 *Rust Owen Lumber Company garage, project, Drummond, Wis., P&E no. 391*

1919 *Minneapolis Business Women's Club, project, Minneapolis, P&E no. 395*

1920 *Union Bottling Works, project, Minneapolis, P&E no. 398*

1920 *Kramer Hotel, project, Mudlava, Ind., P&E no. 400*

Civic Structures

1908 *Soldiers Memorial Arch for C. M. Loring, project, Minneapolis, P&F no. 35*

1909 *City Hall, project, Eau Claire, Wis., P&F no. 65*

1913 *Winona lampposts, project, Winona, Minn., PF&E no. 184*

1913 *Litchfield Pavilion, project, Litchfield, Minn., PF&E no. 207*

1914 *Australian Parliament Buildings competition, project, P&E no. 227; no. 325 (1917)*

1914 *Yale Place street extension, project, Minneapolis, P&E no. 243*

1914 Anoka Open-Air Theater, Anoka, Minn., P&E no. 246

1915 *Le Roy Library, project, Le Roy, Minn., P&E no. 275*

1915 Woodbury County Courthouse, Sioux City, Iowa, P&E no. 276 (with William L. Steele)

1915 Jump River Town Hall, Jump River, Wis., P&E no. 285

1916 *Municipal Auditorium competition, Minneapolis, P&E no. 319*

1916 Kasson Municipal Building, Kasson, Minn., P&E no. 327

Schools

1907 *AKX Sorority, project, Wellesley, Mass., P&F no. 2½*

1907 *Cargill Science Hall, Albert Lea College, project, Albert Lea, Minn., P&F no. 10*

1911 *Rhinelander High School, project, Rhinelander, Wis., PF&E no. 133*

1912 *Sandusky High School, project, Sandusky, Ohio, PF&E no. 138*

1912 *Gratia Countryman women's dormitory, project, Minneapolis, PF&E no. 158*

1918 Helen C. Peirce School, Chicago, P&E no. 362 (completed by Elmslie in 1924)

Religious Structures

1908 *United Brethren Church, project, Minneapolis, P&F no. 19*

1908 Christ Church parish house and chancel, Eau Claire, Wis., P&F no. 24

1909 *Methodist Church, project, Eau Claire, Wis., P&F no. 43*

1909 Stewart Memorial Church, Minneapolis, P&F no. 56

1910 *Saint Paul's Episcopal Church, project, Cedar Rapids, Iowa, PF&E no. 86*

1911 *Christian Church, project, Cedar Rapids, Iowa, PF&E no. 107*

1913 *Parish of St. Anthony rectory, project, Minneapolis, PF&E no. 202*

1913 First Congregational Church community house, Eau Claire, Wis., P&E no. 221

1914 *Third Christian Science Church, project, Minneapolis, P&E no. 250*

1915 Christ Church memorial window, Eau Claire, Wis., P&E no. 287

1915 *Episcopal Church, project, Owen, Wis., P&E no. 289*

1915 *Fourteenth Christian Science Church, project, Chicago, P&E no. 291*

1915 *Tenth Christian Science Church, project, Chicago, P&E no. 292*

1915 Second Christian Science Church light fixtures, location unknown, P&E no. 298

1916 *Institutional Church for Charles O. Alexander (Y.M.C.A.), project, Siang Tang, Hunan, China, P&E no. 310*

1917 *Third Christian Science Church, project, Riverside, Ill., P&E no. 330*

1919 *Rust Owen Lumber Company Church, project, Drummond, Wis., P&E no. 392*

SELECTED BIBLIOGRAPHY

The main source of information for this book was William Gray Purcell. Beginning in the 1930s and continuing into the late 1950s, Purcell systematically went through the firm's commissions, writing down everything he could remember. He also wrote biographical sketches of many members of the firm and its associates. This information was passed along to others, particularly George Grant Elmslie, for comment. These "Parabiographies," as Purcell named them, are found in the William Gray Purcell Papers of the University of Minnesota's Northwest Architectural Archives, along with other papers, photographs, and drawings detailing the firm's work.

Books

Brock, Thomas D. *Shorewood Hills: An Illustrated History.* Madison, Wis.: Village of Shorewood Hills, 1999.

Brooks, H. Allen. *The Prairie School: Frank Lloyd Wright and His Midwest Contemporaries.* New York: Norton, 1972.

——. *Prairie School Architecture: Studies from "The Western Architect."* Toronto: University of Toronto Press, 1983.

Gebhard, David, and Tom Martinson. *A Guide to the Architecture of Minnesota.* Minneapolis: University of Minnesota Press, 1977.

Hammons, Mark. "Purcell and Elmslie, Architects." In *Minnesota 1900: Art and Life on the Upper Mississippi, 1890–1915,* edited by Michael Conforti. Toronto: Associated University Press and Minneapolis Institute of Arts, 1994.

Millett, Larry. *The Curve of the Arch: The Story of Louis Sullivan's Owatonna Bank.* St. Paul: Minnesota Historical Society Press, 1985.

Mucha, Jiri. *Alphonse Mucha: His Life and Art.* London: Heinemann, 1966.

Olivarez, Jennifer Komar. *Progressive Design in the Midwest: The Purcell-Cutts House and the Prairie School Collection at the Minneapolis Institute of Arts.* Minneapolis: Minneapolis Institute of Arts, 2000.

Roth, Leland M. *Shingle Styles: Innovation and Tradition in American Architecture, 1874 to 1982.* New York: Abrams, 1999.

Other Sources

Hammons, Mark. *Purcell and Elmslie Architects: Architecture in the Spirit of Democracy.* www.organica.org/purcellandelmslie.htm.

Hanson, Krista Finstad. "A Prairie School Legacy." *American Bungalow,* April 15, 1998, pages 28–33.

Minneapolis Institute of Arts. *Unified Vision: The Architecture and Design of the Prairie School.* www.artsmia.org/unified-vision.

Moran, Maya. "A Prairie Bungalow by the Sea." *American Bungalow,* April 15, 1997, pages 26–31.

Northwest Architectural Archives, University of Minnesota. William Gray Purcell Papers and Purcell and Elmslie Architectural Records, "Purcell and Elmslie Biographical Notes," 1949. http://special.lib.umn.edu/manuscripts/WGP/N3WGPintro.html.

Purcell, William Gray. "Parabiographies," ca. 1930s to 1950s. William Gray Purcell Papers, vols. 1907 to 1920. Northwest Architectural Archives, University of Minnesota.

ACKNOWLEDGMENTS

I am deeply grateful to all the homeowners who so graciously opened their doors to us. I am also indebted to Barbara Bezat at the University of Minnesota's Northwest Architectural Archives for her willing assistance and vast knowledge; Krista Finstad Hanson for sharing her research with me; and also H. Allen Brooks, the late David Gebhard, and Mark Hammons, whose research on the Prairie School and Purcell and Elmslie have contributed so greatly to understanding this architectural movement.

Special thanks go to my dear friend Diane Maddex, president of Archetype Press; Robert Wiser, for his beautiful design; Christian Korab, for his exquisite photographs; and Alan Rapp, Bridget Watson Payne, and Sara Schneider of Chronicle Books.

In addition, the following individuals and two organizations offered invaluable assistance: Bruce Albinson, Nancy Albrecht, Allan and Ginna Amis, David and Martha Anderson, Rolf T. Anderson, Lynn Barnhouse, Max M. Burger, Jean Chesley, Steven Corcoran, Thomas S. and Gerri Crane, James and Linda Fahey, Frances and Henry Fogel, Karla and Bill Forsyth, Jan Fox, Bob Glancy, Suzanne and James P. Greenawalt, JoAnn Hanson, David Heide, Char Henn, Kathy Holm, Richelle Huff, Charles Koch, Beth Larson, Terri and Allan Lieder, Paul Lenz, Ruth Makinen, Michael McCarthy, Gardner Miller, Minneapolis Institute of Arts (bequest of Anson Cutts), James and Murel O'Connell, Tom Oliphant, Jennifer Komar Olivarez, Constance Olser, Joanne Opgenorth, Robert and Susan Pitts, Devra and Mark Rich, James Sandberg, Kim and Tim Taylor, Peter and Karen Thill, Mary Tomashek, Ellen and Gordon Tully, Mark Walbran, Corine Wegener, and Wells Fargo Bank, Owatonna, Minnesota.

I also want to thank John Legler as well as my dear friend Pedro E. Guerrero for his support and good cheer.   —*Dixie Legler*

Display illustrations: Spine, Atkinson House stencil. Case binding: Beebe House stencil frieze. Front endpapers: Powers House fireplace detail. Page 1: Purcell-Cutts House sidelight. Pages 2–3: Bradley summer bungalow, Woods Hole, Massachusetts. Pages 4–5 background: Parker House doorway. Pages 6–7: Goodnow House window and door. Pages 8–9: Bradley House, Madison, Wisconsin, new fireplace and skylight. Pages 10–11: Goosman House exterior detail and front window. Pages 12–13: Goodnow House rendering by Purcell and Elmslie. Pages 30–31: Powers House dining room rendering by Gustav Weber. Pages 46–47: Carlson House rendering by Purcell and Elmslie. Page 192: Heitman House sketch by William Gray Purcell. Back endpapers: Bradley summer bungalow, Woods Hole, Massachusetts, living room ceiling detail.

All photographs and original digital mastering by Christian Korab except as follows: Illustrations on the spine and pages 12–13, 14, 15, 21, 22, 23, 24, 26, 30–31, 34–35, 36, 45, 46–47, and 192 are from the William Gray Purcell Papers, Northwest Architectural Archives, University of Minnesota Libraries, Minneapolis. The photograph on page 29 is by Alexander Vertikoff. Photographs on pages 176–79 are by Scot Zimmerman. The case binding and spine stencil illustrations were adapted by Robert L. Wiser.

Library of Congress Cataloging-in-Publication Data available.
ISBN-10: 0-8118-5041-2
ISBN-13: 978-0-8118-5041-4

Produced by Archetype Press, Inc.
Diane Maddex, Project Director
Robert L. Wiser, Designer

Manufactured in China

Distributed in Canada by Raincoast Books
9050 Shaughnessy Street
Vancouver, British Columbia V6P 6E5

10   9   8   7   6   5   4   3   2   1

Chronicle Books LLC
85 Second Street
San Francisco, California 94105
www.chroniclebooks.com